# How to Deal with How You Feel

JAMES MERRITT

HARVEST HOUSE PUBLISHERS
EUGENE. OREGON

**How to Deal with How You Feel**
Copyright © 2022 by James Merritt
Published by Harvest House Publishers
Eugene, Oregon 97408
www.harvesthousepublishers.com

ISBN 978-0-7369-8534-5 (pbk.)
ISBN 978-0-7369-8535-2 (eBook)

Library of Congress Control Number: 2021949963

# CONTENTS

# EMOTION COMMOTION

I recently began seeing a therapist, which I must admit made me feel a little awkward. You see, I've been a pastor for more than 45 years, so I'm usually the one performing the counseling, not the one receiving it. People often come to me for help when they're feeling sad or mad or guilty. They seek me out when they're overwhelmed by disappointment or disagreement or disease or death and they can't seem to control all the emotions these experiences have dredged up. As a pastor, my job is to help them process what they're feeling in a biblical way.

But now I've ended up on the other side of the desk. I'm the one seeking advice, not doling it out, and this is a new experience for me. My counselor, like all good counselors, has helped me deal with my feelings—honestly confront the emotions churning inside of me. Conversations with him have uncovered hidden insecurities, catalogued anxieties, and revealed unspoken jealousies I didn't even know I was harboring. We've worked to process my anger—something I've had to deal with all of my life—and to confront the guilt I sometimes feel.

Maybe you can relate. An early 2021 report by the American Psychological Association revealed that 84 percent of American adults had recently felt anxious (47 percent), sad (44 percent), angry (39 percent), or some other powerful emotion associated with prolonged stress such as experienced in a pandemic.[1] But we can't blame all challenging emotions on COVID-19. Two in three adults surveyed said that the "number of issues America is facing" was "overwhelming to them."[2]

But you don't need a study to know an emotion commotion is going on in America. The pandemic and America's other challenges certainly contributed to the results in that report, but for all kinds of reasons, everywhere you look you'll witness the burning fires of anger, the sneak attacks of anxiety, the furrowed wrinkles of worry, and the sweat of stress running down foreheads.

And let's not pretend these emotions are only "out there" and not inside us as well. Perhaps you're a single mom angry with your ex-husband—the one who left you for another woman and is trying to dodge paying child support. Maybe you're depressed because you lost your dream job when your company downsized and it's shredded your sense of self-worth. You might feel anxious because you're awaiting the results of a biopsy, and the worry is compounded by fear you'll receive bad news. Or perhaps you feel bitter toward someone you once trusted as a friend who betrayed you and couldn't care less about your hurt.

Feelings are not the most important thing about us,[3] but they are one of the more powerful drivers in our lives. So how should we deal with our emotions? Well, first let me tell you how *not* to deal with them and then what to do instead.

## AVOID EXTREMES
## WITH YOUR EMOTIONS

Whatever their cause, when it comes to the feelings we'll address in this book—stress, worry, anxiety, depression, fear, loneliness, jealousy, anger, bitterness, and guilt...what we might call "life takers"—many people tend to gravitate toward one of two extremes. In an article adapted from his book *Untangled Emotions*, Alasdair Groves writes about "emotional obsession" and how some people adopt an "emotions are nothing" stance.[4] I express this idea by saying people tend to either *ignore* their emotions or *idolize* them. Both paths are extreme and problematic.

### Ignoring feelings

Some people strive to, as Groves says, "keep a stiff upper lip," a saying derived from the physiological fact that a trembling of the upper lip is often the first visible sign of emotion. So, the thinking goes, one should stiffen their upper lip to hide emotion. These people resist feeling what they consider to be "unfeel-able" feelings churning inside of them. When an acquaintance, coworker, or neighbor asks, "How have you been?" many people reflexively respond with "Fine" or some benign equivalent. But if they told the truth, they'd say, "I'm mad as a hornet" or "I'm down in the dumps" or "I'm worried to death."

Maybe we're afraid of admitting our vulnerabilities, but here's the truth: These emotions are not bad; they're not a sign of weakness or unhealth. Emotions are good, and some of them are even godly. God created us with a mind to think, yes, but also with a heart to feel. As the late British pastor and author John Stott wrote, "We are to be neither such emotional Christians that we never think, nor such intellectual Christians that we never feel. No, God made us human beings, and human beings are by creation both rational and emotional."[5]

Whenever I had a meltdown as a child, my dad told me, "Big boys don't cry." Since every little boy wants to be a "big boy," I'd muster enough resolve to turn off the waterworks and dry my eyes. Years later, I repeated this phrase to my eldest son when he fell and skinned his knee. It must've made an impression on him, because when he grew up he went to law school and now jokes, "Big boys don't cry; they sue."

The truth is both boys and girls should cry sometimes, whether they're big or small. While great poker players may be good at hiding their emotions, life is not a card game. We humans are creatures with feelings, and at the right time and in the right place and in the right way it's appropriate and healthy to express even the most challenging emotions. If we reflexively avoid or ignore those feelings, we do so at our peril.

Christians like me know that even Jesus Christ was an emotional person. And according to the record of his life in the New Testament Gospels, he regularly displayed an array of emotions. Jesus exhibited burning anger toward religious hypocrites and moneychangers who were extorting the poor in the temple courts. He experienced such stress in the garden of Gethsemane that he literally sweat drops of blood. And on the cross, abandoned by nearly all his followers, Jesus felt overwhelming loneliness when even his heavenly Father turned his back on him. You may be familiar with his cross-bound cry: "My God, my God, why have you forsaken me?" (Matthew 27:46).

So if you're an emotional person, congratulations. You're in good company.

### Idolizing feelings

Idolizing feelings is the other extreme. Many people today are hyper-focused on their emotions. They believe that expressing them—anywhere and at any time and in any way—is good. Groves says some people think they "need to express yourself at any cost," and that's why they "value 'getting it off your chest,' 'letting off steam,' 'just being honest,' and so on."[6] They call this "authenticity," but sometimes it's just poor judgment.

If you don't believe me, check your social media feeds, which no doubt too often include a torrent of uncontrolled emotional posts that keep the water in the pot of human feelings relentlessly boiling. Seven in ten Americans use social media,[7] and so many of them seem ready and willing to share their unfiltered feelings. This tendency is just as unhealthy as the impulse to stuff all your emotions inside and pretend they don't exist.

## LEARN TO CONTROL YOUR EMOTIONS

Rather than ignore feelings or idolize your emotions, it's crucial that you learn to control them. If you don't control them, they'll control you. Uncontrolled emotions can ruin your marriage and harm your children. They can destroy your friendships and ruin your job prospects. They can even erode your health.

In recent years doctors have learned about what's called the mind-body connection, and we now know a person's emotional life can have profound effects on their physical well-being. In his book *Deadly Emotions*, Dr. Don Colbert shares what medical science has found:

- "Certain emotions release hormones into the physical body that, in turn, can trigger the development of a host of diseases...

- Researchers have directly and scientifically linked emotions to hypertension, cardiovascular disease, and diseases related to the immune system...

- Research has linked emotions such as depression to an increased risk of developing cancer and heart disease. Emotions such as anxiety and fear have shown a direct tie to heart palpitations, mitral valve prolapse, irritable bowel syndrome, and tension headaches."[8]

The stakes for this conversation about emotions, then, could not be higher.

## LEARN WHAT GOD
## SAYS ABOUT EMOTIONS

I love my Christian counselor, but I'm more concerned about what God's Word teaches about my emotions than I am about what any therapist thinks about them. That's why I recently turned to the Bible to explore what it says about emotions, and I learned that the God who created us to feel has a lot to say about the matter.

Feelings are subjective, and so, just like shifting sand, they can change without warning. But when you build your life on the solid rock of God's truth, you can rule your emotions rather than allowing them to rule you. We must not ignore them or idolize them; we must learn to manage them. And we do that by heeding what God says about them. The ancient wisdom found in Scripture lays out how to *control* our feelings so they don't *consume* us.

This book, then, not only outlines God's blueprint for how to deal with your emotions but includes good news about the "life givers" of faith, joy, gratitude, contentment, and hope. Some of the material is from books I've previously published, but after my recent dive into the Word, I've tried to give each illustration, story, example, comment, explanation, and thought a fresh and still biblical perspective.

Now, let's explore how you can deal with how you feel—and do it successfully!

PART ONE

# LIFE TAKERS

# SOAR LIKE AN EAGLE

*Rule number one is, don't sweat the small stuff.*
*Rule number two is, it's all small stuff.*

**ROBERT ELIOT**

Following the American Civil War, Ulysses S. Grant and William T. Sherman were two of the most popular men in the northern half of the United States. They'd been the leading generals of the Union army and had received much praise in the press. Grant went on to become the president of the United States.

Many people believed Sherman had a clear path to the White House as well, but when he was asked in 1884 if he would run for president, he famously replied, "I will not accept if nominated and will not serve if elected." That became known as the "Sherman pledge."[1] If the general were alive today, he would probably make the same statement but even more emphatically.

The presidency of the United States is considered perhaps the most stressful job on earth. In fact, journalist John Dickerson wrote a book about the American presidency titled *The Hardest Job in the World*. Just think about the duties of the office:

- Chief Executive
- Head of Government
- Commander-in-Chief
- Head of State
- Chief Diplomat
- Chief Legislator
- Political Party Leader[2]

Talk about stressful! And no man or woman could possibly represent the country's current population of nearly 332 million with all the different opinions and interests its citizens have. Don't you wonder why anyone would *ever* want this job? How can anyone manage an executive branch of 2 million employees, which doesn't even include the largest military in the world?

It shouldn't surprise us that a study published by the *British Medical Journal* found that such leaders "after adjusting for a candidate's age and life expectancy…were found to live 2.7 years less [than the runners up] and have a 23% higher risk of premature death."[3] Even the most powerful person on this planet knows what stress is like every second of every day.

The president is not alone. No matter what age, sex, ethnicity, or religion we are, none of us are immune to the stress virus. According to the American Institute of Stress in a 2014 study,

- "77 percent of people experience stress that affects their physical health.

- 73 percent of people have stress that impacts their mental health.

- 48 percent of people have trouble sleeping because of stress."[4]

Furthermore, according to the Global Organization for Stress as of May 2020, about half of all Americans' levels of stress have been getting worse. In their study, they found that…

- 75 percent of Americans had "experienced moderate to high stress levels in the past month."

- Stress was "the number one health concern of high school students."

- 80 percent of people felt "stress at work."[5]

And a 2020 Harris Poll survey tells us that 83 percent of Americans said "the future of our nation" was "a significant source of stress."[6]

So none of this should surprise us, especially as of this writing. America has been in the perfect storm of the COVID-19 pandemic, economic uncertainty, traumatic events related to racism and racial tensions, changing foreign policy—and it's still in the aftermath of the most divisive, political election in decades. Stress is taking an incredible toll on us.

You might say stress taxes us more than the IRS. After all, even back in the 1990s, 75 to 90 percent of all doctor office visits were for stress-related ailments,[7] and today "illnesses and injuries associated with stress are estimated to cost more than $300 billion annually. This includes losses from absenteeism, employee turnover and lost productivity as well as direct legal, medical and insurance fees."[8] More, "the lifetime prevalence of an emotional disorder is more than 50%, often due to chronic, untreated stress reaction."[9]

As I mentioned earlier, the mind-body connection tells us unmediated chronic stress is a major contributor to health challenges. They include heart problems, high blood pressure, headaches, mental conditions—and they feed into the emotion of anxiety.[10] In his 2016 book

*Impossible People*, Os Guinness wrote, "We now live in a world of 'speed, stuff and stress.'" That makes our days ones of juggling time and multitasking. "We are all rats in the rat race," he also said, and we have moved from the survival of the fittest to the "survival of the fastest."[11]

Early in my career, I went through a period of stress so intense that I began to lose my hair and developed high blood pressure. Today, both my head and my medicine cabinet testify to how bad it was! But what is stress? Basically, it's the gap between what we face and what we *think* we can face. It's the difference in what we believe we *must* do versus what we believe we *can* do. We can call it the "stress factor"—the canyon between the "ought to" and what we think we "can't do." Dr. Colbert put it simply when he wrote, "A person's stress level has to do with what a person believes."[12]

## LESSONS FROM ISAIAH

Almost three millennia ago, a prophet named Isaiah gave some advice to his nation, which was suffering under crushing stress. Bear with me as I give you a quick history lesson.

At the height of its power, Israel was the greatest nation on earth. It was ruled by two great kings, David and then his son, Solomon. After Solomon died, the nation split in two for reasons we don't have the space to go into.

Of the 12 tribes of Israel, ten of them formed the Northern Kingdom of Israel and two formed the Southern Kingdom of Judah. Both kingdoms fell into spiritual decline, rebelling against God and his laws. God sent prophets to both kingdoms to call them back to spiritual renewal, but they refused to listen. This spiritual decline lasted 350 years, until, finally, the Northern Kingdom of Israel fell to the Assyrians in 722 BC and they were led into exile.

The Southern Kingdom of Judah fell to the Babylonians 136 years later. The temple was destroyed, and the city of Jerusalem was left desolate. The Northern Kingdom of Israel was lost forever, but a remnant from the Southern Kingdom of Judah was allowed to return to the promised land to reestablish the Jewish homeland. That in effect is the end of the history in the Old Testament.

As Jerusalem was under siege, God revealed to the prophet Jeremiah that the nation of Judah would fall. They would be taken into exile, the city would be leveled, and Judah would be no more. Jeremiah thought there was nothing left to do except wait on the trouble coming. The future was bleak, and time was short. The dam had broken, and nothing could stop the flood of God's judgment about to come on this nation. God's people would face the most difficult, trying, discouraging, faith-testing season in all of their history. The promised land, Jerusalem, and the temple were going to be lost, captured, and destroyed. The unrelenting pressure of stress was unbearable.

Everything has a stress limit. For example, trucks are monitored at weigh stations to ensure their cargo doesn't exceed the designated limit. Humans have stress limits, too, and I'm sure Isaiah had reached his. The Holmes-Rahe Life Stress Inventory assigns points to stress-causing events. The death of a spouse is 100 points, a divorce is 73, a major illness is 53, and being fired is 47. Strangely, a vacation is 13 points, and celebrating a major holiday like Christmas is 12! An accumulation of more than 150 points in a year can lead to a major health breakdown.[13]

How many points do you suppose Isaiah had accumulated? Well, whatever it was, God knows our stress limits, he knew Isaiah's stress limit, and he knew the stress limits of the people to whom Isaiah prophesied. So he gave his prophet a reminder of who he is and what he can do.

Isaiah 40 gives us a divine prescription for stress that comes from the heart of God. So when life becomes unbearable, the storm gets too strong, your rope of hope has been cut in half, and you feel like throwing in the towel, here's what you should do to meet stress: Look up at the unequaled God, listen to the unlimited God, and linger with the unfailing God.

## LOOK UP AT THE UNEQUALED GOD

This may sound simplistic, but when you're stressed out, go outside after dark and just look up. That's what Isaiah told the nation of Israel to do, "Lift up your eyes and look to the heavens" (Isaiah 40:26).

In other words, he said, "Get out of your fetal position, quit walking the floor, go outside, and look up." Why? Because he preceded his directive with, "'To whom will you compare me? Or who is my equal?' says the Holy One" (verse 25). And then he followed with, "Who created all these? He who brings out the starry host one by one and calls forth each of them by name. Because of his great power and mighty strength, not one of them is missing" (verse 26).

This God—Isaiah's God, the Bible's God—is an unequaled God. You can put every other so-called "god" together and they would never equal even the one true God's smallest toenail. And the proof isn't "in the pudding"; it's in the stars. But when the ancient Israelites heard Isaiah's words, they had no idea what incredible words they were.

On a mission trip in Zambia, I was taking a boat up the Zambezi River to speak to pastors who were coming from many miles around. After a four-hour ride, we were deep into the African jungle. That first night we were sleeping in a tent when I woke up. I slipped outside, and what I saw was breathtaking. I had never seen so many stars in my life! It was as though they had become rabbits and multiplied while I slept! But the reason I could see so many stars was that we weren't around any electric lights or pollution. We just had a clear, clean sky.

Astronomers tell us only a little over 9,000 stars are visible to the naked eye, but that's only about one to the hundredth quintillionth of stars out there. A quintillion is a one followed by 20 zeroes. They also estimate the number of stars in the universe is about three septillion. That's a three with 24 zeroes after it. That number is constantly expanding. And every single second those three septillion stars put out roughly the same amount of energy as a trillion atom bombs. We now see infrared images of galaxies we didn't even know existed, estimated at about 12 million light-years away.

And Isaiah said God calls every one of them by name![14]

To put it another way, astronomers estimate that 100 billion to 400 billion stars are in our galaxy, and now the Hubble Space Telescope indicates there may be two trillion other galaxies in the universe with who knows how many stars. Yet God says, *Not one of them is missing by my power and my mighty strength.* Not one runaway, renegade star is anywhere in this universe.

What is my point? If God has such a firm grasp on the universe, don't you think he can handle whatever is causing you stress? If God can keep stars in their orbits and planets in their place and make an entire universe run like a Swiss watch, then when he says to you *I've got this*, you can believe it.

## LISTEN TO THE UNLIMITED GOD

The prophet Isaiah would have been a fantastic therapist because his practical advice on how to handle stress is both wise and timely. First he said to open your eyes and look up. Then he said to open your ears and listen: "Do you not know? Have you not heard? The LORD is the everlasting God, the Creator of the ends of the earth. He will not grow tired or weary, and his understanding no one can fathom. He gives strength to the weary and increases the power of the weak" (Isaiah 40:28-29).

What is it the people should have known? They should have known what they had repeatedly heard from the Word of God. They should have known what other prophets had preached. They should have heard what other prophets had written about God.

### Our God is the all-knowing, all-seeing, all-hearing, ever-present God.

God is not limited by time or space. He is the creator of the ends of the earth and both the creator and the controller of everything, everywhere. The nation of Israel should have known that. Yet just before this reminder in verses 28 and 29, Isaiah has to say to them, "Why do you complain, Jacob? Why do you say, Israel, 'My way is hidden from the LORD; my cause is disregarded by my God'?" (verse 27).

Yet the nation *is* under tremendous stress. They're about to be taken over by a pagan people, to be removed from their own country, and to see everything they love destroyed. They were asking the questions people commonly ask under duress: *Does God know what's happening? Does God hear my prayers? Does God even care?*

We can fall into the trap of thinking we can put God on our clock, and then he has to work according to our timetable. We try to put him in a box. We think he has to do what we want him to do, at the time we want him to do it, and in the way we want him to do it. And we really want that to happen when we don't understand what's going on or how to handle it.

But then in verse 28, Isaiah reminds them and us, "[God's] understanding no one can fathom." That can be translated, "There is no limit to his understanding."[15] Only one true know-it-all exists in the universe—God! We might not always know what we're doing, but God always knows what he's doing. We might not understand why things are happening the way they are, but that doesn't mean there isn't a reason.

### Our God is the loving and all-powerful God.

Of course, we would never have stress if we didn't have stressful problems. So we wonder, *If God loves me, why does he allow me to have stressful problems?*

Well, think about this: If you could get rid of earthquakes, would you? Before you answer too quickly, you may need to know that earthquakes are important for life.

> Earthquakes are the earth's way of releasing energy stored in plate tectonics as they move. If plate tectonics could not move, the world would look dramatically different, with no mountains and distinctly smaller oceans. As plate tectonics move, it naturally cycles materials from the mantle of the earth. The seafloor that new material creates harbors thousands of species of plants and animals, which themselves play important roles in the human ecosystem by doing things like absorbing carbon dioxide and releasing oxygen through photosynthesis. Without the movement that allows earthquakes, none of this could occur on the earth.[16]

God knows how to use anything for our good, including earthquakes! Maybe that's why the French priest Jacques Marie-Louis Monsabré, who lived in the nineteenth and early twentieth centuries, is widely said to have declared, "If God would concede me his omnipotence for 24 hours, you would see how many changes I would make in the world. But if he gave me his wisdom, too, I would leave things as they are."

If your stress has just worn you out, if you're exhausted and ready to pack it in and hang it up, remember the God who is of unlimited understanding and unlimited strength. He doesn't grow tired or weary. He never gives out, takes a break, or needs a vacation. He's never confused and never perplexed.

Stop right now and listen to the God who has told us he will give strength to the weary and increase the power of the weak. Listen to the God whose own strength has no limit and who can handle any situation.

## LINGER WITH THE UNFAILING GOD

If you're like me, you're a fixer by nature. When people come to me with problems, I'm not always the best listener because I just want to fix their problem. And when I turn to God in my own stressful times, I admit I want him to fix the problem and fix it quickly.

Be honest. When you're under tremendous stress, you want the problem fixed too. So the first few words of this next verse from Isaiah might not make you happy at first: "They who wait for the LORD shall renew their strength" (Isaiah 40:31 ESV).

Now, if, for example, you're about to lose your job, you're probably thinking what I would probably be thinking: *Wait? What do you mean? We're about to be shut down, and I'm about to be unemployed. The wolves are at the door. The end is near, and you want me to wait?*

But *this* waiting doesn't mean you do nothing, curl up in a fetal position, walk the floor, or bite your fingernails down to the quick waiting for something to happen. Waiting on the Lord means waiting *with* the Lord. You set aside your stress for the moment and take time to get alone with God. You sit at his feet and allow him to build your faith and your trust as you once again listen to the great God he is.

While you're waiting on God, you're simply telling him this: *Lord, I'm totally dependent on you. I'm helpless and hopeless without you. But I have an absolutely unshakable confidence that you are the everlasting God, that you will work this out for my good, that your purpose will be fulfilled in my life, and that your will is going to be done in such a way that I get the good and you get the glory.*

God never said waiting on him would be easy, but consider that, as you wait, he wants to give you good, he wants to give you good work, and he will give you strength.

### Expect God to give you his good.

Here's a personal story that illustrates why I can testify to the truth of the saying *Good things come to those who wait*.

When I asked Teresa to marry me, she wasn't too excited about my proposal. I can understand that to an extent because I proposed to her on our second date! Two weeks went by, and on Labor Day I arrived at her home and spent the entire day with her. Her intention was to break things off with me because she wasn't ready to get serious with anyone. The whole time she kept trying to tell me to hit the trail, but she just couldn't do it.

Every time we visit her mother and we walk by a pillar on her front porch, I remember what happened before I left that day. Teresa asked me to give her some time to think and pray. I said, "I'm willing to give you all the space you need and all the time you want because I believe you're God's mate for me. So I'm going to get in my car and leave. I'm not going to call you, write you, or visit you. I'm just going to pray, and if I'm right, God will show you. And if I'm wrong, God will show you that too."

I'll never forget what Teresa did then. She got literally nose to nose, and with the smile of a Cheshire cat she said, "You'll be back!" The truth of the matter is I probably would have until she said that. My male ego and pride kicked in, and I told her, "Pigs will fly and elephants will become ballerinas before you'll hear from me again!"

I didn't go back, but I waited and waited and waited to hear from her—for two whole weeks. And I will tell you those were the longest two weeks of my life. Every day I didn't hear from her, my hopes sank deeper and deeper. But I prayed like I had never prayed before and just kept trusting and obeying, believing God had my good and Teresa's in mind.

My heart started pounding when I got a letter from her because I thought it was a Dear John letter. Maybe the good God wanted for me and for Teresa wasn't the good I'd expected. But instead the letter was a *Please call me; I miss you terribly* letter. The rest, as they say, is history.

Waiting on the Lord also means serving him.

### Expect God to give you good work.

When you're stressed out and you don't know what to do, do what you do know to do—stay in the presence of God and continue serving him. Waiting on the Lord doesn't mean just waiting on him to do something for us; we must continue to do what we need to do for him. I remember pastoring in Mississippi and feeling strongly that I was to go back to Georgia. It was almost four months before God began to move in that direction, but I continued to work as if I would be there the rest of my life. I learned that God is always faithful to us wherever we are. We are to be faithful to him wherever we are until he moves our "wherever."

### Expect God to give you strength.

When you wait for the Lord, something happens, which we see in the second half of Isaiah 40:31 (ESV): "They who wait for the LORD shall renew their strength."

The Hebrew word in that verse for "renew" means "exchange."[17] If you give God your stress, he will exchange it for his strength. You can exchange your weariness for his power. The Christian life is not just a changed life; it's an exchanged life. Turn to the greatest strength coach who has ever lived and he will strengthen you.

God is able to handle any storm, and because of his strength, he also says in verse 31, "They will soar on wings like eagles." But what do eagles have to do with stress?

Eagles are the only birds that love the storm. When all other birds try to flee from the storm and hide its fierceness, eagles fly into it and will use the wind of the storm to rise higher in a matter of seconds. They use the pressure of the storm to glide higher without having to use their own energy. They are able to do this because God has created them uniquely with an ability to lock their wings in a fixed position in the midst of the fierce storm winds.[18]

God has uniquely created eagles with an ability to lock their massive wings in a fixed position in the midst of the fiercest storm. Their wings have more than 7,000 feathers. They're like the wings of an airplane, and the birds can use the thermal drafts caused by the storm to lift off and fly up to an altitude of 10,000 feet! And not only can they fly higher, but they can fly faster. An eagle can reach a speed of 50 miles per hour, and in a storm it can get up to 100 miles per hour. Eagles don't fear storms because they soar above them, and because they do, they can fly higher, see farther, and go faster.

Now, what is the message here? When we're under stress, God wants us to be with him above the storm. He wants us to see our storms and troubles from his point of view. What is his point of view? *I am over every storm. I am in control of the thunder you hear and the lightning you see. As long as you fly with me, you don't have to fear any storm.*

Then in the same verse 31, he follows with, "They will run and not grow weary, they will walk and not be faint." It's one thing to fly above a storm, but you still have to go through the storm. What God is simply saying is this: *Just keep putting one foot in front of the other, and as you do, don't look down at the ground; look up at the sky. If you wait on me and serve me, you will fly higher than the storm, run faster in the storm, and walk longer through the storm.*

———

Possibly no United States president in the last 50 years has faced more stress or a greater challenge than George W. Bush did on September 11, 2001. But he led our nation through that storm, and he showed us we could soar above it. That probably explains why, when in 2005 he stepped to the platform to take the oath of office for his second term, his hand on the Bible, he'd chosen Isaiah 40:31 for that Bible to be opened to. It was highlighted, and it was his personal wish. "Those who hope in the LORD will renew their strength. They will soar on wings like eagles; they will run and not grow weary, they will walk and not be faint."

So remember, when you're in the storm of stress, look up to an unequaled God, listen to the unlimited God, and linger with the unfailing God. Then soar above that storm like an eagle.

# PUT WORRIES WHERE THEY BELONG

*The reason why worry kills more people than work is that more people worry than work.*

**ROBERT FROST**

In this chapter we'll tackle the particular emotion that's my Achilles' heel. It's the biggest emotion I deal with and have dealt with all of my life. It's called worry.

I tend to be a worrywart at times. And when I'm not worried, I get worried that I should be worried. But worry is a common emotion that afflicts many people. If I asked you how you're feeling today, and you were honest, you might answer, "I'm worried." Gallup's annual Global Emotions Report is from a survey of more than 150,000 people around the world, and in 2019 it stated that "45% of Americans said they felt a lot of worry, in comparison to a 39% global average."[1]

Sociologists and psychologists across the landscape freely admit that America's mental health is not healthy, and worry is a big reason. A 2017 article titled "America's Insomnia Problem Is Even Worse Than Before the Great Recession" found that "Americans are more stressed than ever—and for many of them, their bank accounts are to blame." It went on to say that 65 percent of Americans were "losing sleep over money issues," and the "most common stressor" was health care or insurance bills, "followed by saving for retirement." Stress over how to pay off student loans, make mortgage payments, and pay on credit cards came next.[2]

And if that wasn't enough to steal our beauty rest, we now—as of this writing—have a global pandemic to worry about. Even as vaccines against COVID-19 had become widely available by June 2021 in the United States, Gallup reported that 66 percent of Americans said they were still either very or somewhat worried about exposure to the virus.[3] A new, more transmissible variant of COVID-19 had no doubt added to that worry.

## WHAT WORRY IS NOT

Now, before we talk about what worry is, let's talk about what worry is not. Worry is not concern. We should all be concerned about the spiritual condition of our nation—and our neighborhood. We should be concerned about our children's safety—and their education. We should be concerned about saving money for retirement or a rainy day. But there's a difference between concern and worry. It might help to think of it as Harold Stephens did: "A worried person sees a problem, and a concerned person solves a problem."[4]

Fortunately, Jesus had a lot to say about worry. A big portion of the greatest sermon ever preached in the history of the world—from Matthew chapters 5, 6, and 7 and commonly called Jesus' Sermon on the Mount—was devoted to worry and how we can conquer it. And in Isaiah 43:18, the Israelites were told, "Do not dwell on the past."

We need to put yesterday's worries in their proper place, put today's worries in their proper position, and put tomorrow's worries in proper perspective.

## PUT YESTERDAY'S WORRIES
## IN THEIR PROPER PLACE

Jesus repeats the phrase *do not worry* three times in Matthew 6:

- Therefore I tell you, do not worry (verse 25).
- So do not worry (verse 31).
- Therefore do not worry (verse 34).

Once is enough, but when Jesus says something three times, we know how much he means it.

Some of us worry about yesterday. We're worried about the fender bender we were involved in yesterday or the big mistake we made at work yesterday. But consider how you can use the past to help you face the present and look to the future, how you can use yesterday to help you with today and tomorrow when it comes to worry.

Here's a simple question: You're here now, aren't you?

As of right now, you've survived whatever you're worried about from the past. You may be bruised, beaten, and battered, but you're still here, still breathing, still talking, and still living. There's only one reason for that: God got you here. So if he got you through yesterday, don't you think he can take care of you today?

When we read the Old Testament, it's amazing to see how God used the past to teach the nation of Israel how they should not worry about the present or the future. As we discussed in this book's chapter on stress, the prophet Isaiah was preaching to the nation of Israel in dark days. They were facing an enemy that would eventually defeat them and take them into captivity. Both their present and their future looked really dim, but listen to God's message through Isaiah's words: "Listen to me, you descendants of Jacob, all the remnant of the people of Israel, you *whom I have upheld since your birth, and have carried since you were born*" (Isaiah 46:3, emphasis mine).

God is letting you know that from the moment you were conceived in your mother's womb, he was taking care of you. When you came out of your mother's womb, he was taking care of you. You wouldn't be here today if he wasn't taking care of you. When you didn't even know he existed, he was taking care of you. Listen to what he goes on to say in verse 4: "Even to your old age and gray hairs I am he, I am he who will sustain you. I have made you and I will carry you; I will sustain you and I will rescue you." So in verse 3 God is saying, *Before you were born, I took care of you, and now that you're here I'm taking care of you.* Then in verse 4 he fast-forwards to the end of life and says, *When you're old, I'll take care of you then as well.*

Your life is like two bookends. From the moment you were conceived, God was there. Throughout your life, God is there. And at the end of your life, God will still be there—taking care of you.

If you're worried about something from yesterday right now, put that worry in its proper place. God has been faithful in the past, and because he never changes, he is faithful in the present and will be faithful in the future.

Heed the sage advice of American philosopher Ralph Waldo Emerson, who in a letter to his daughter gave these words of wisdom: "Each new day is too dear, with its hopes and invitations, to waste a moment on yesterdays."[5]

## PUT TODAY'S WORRY IN ITS PROPER POSITION

Let's focus on the first statement Jesus makes about worry in Matthew 6: "Do not worry about your life, what you will eat or drink; or about your body, what you will wear. Is not life more than food, and the body more than clothes?" (verse 25).

Obviously, he's not talking about worrying yesterday, because yesterday is gone. He's talking about worrying today. After all, worry always occurs today. He also knows that just telling us not to worry wouldn't stop us from worrying, so in verse 6 he gives us two simple illustrations to show that we can depend on God to take care of today.

First he says, *Just look outside your window*: "Look at the birds of the air; they do not sow or reap or store away in barns, and yet your heavenly Father feeds them. Are you not much more valuable than they?" (verse 26).

Here's a question: Have you ever seen a worried bird? Never in veterinary history has a bird been treated for hypertension or stroke. I mean, think about it. Worry is so worthless that it's not even for the birds!

I came upon some facts I think tell us why Jesus specifically talked about birds. Ornithologists (people who study birds) have identified at least 18,000 species of birds, and today an estimated 200 to 400 billion birds are in the world. "Compared to five billion people, this amounts to between 40 to 60 birds per person!"[6] So if God can daily take care of all those birds, don't you think he can take care of you?

If you aren't into birds, maybe you're into flowers. Jesus goes on to say this in verses 28 through 30:

> Why do you worry about clothes? See how the flowers of the field grow. They do not labor or spin. Yet I tell you that not even Solomon in all his splendor was dressed like one of these. If that is how God clothes the grass of the field, which is here today and tomorrow is thrown into the fire, will he not much more clothe you—you of little faith?

I have never seen a flower break into a sweat. I've never seen a flower pacing a flowerbed. Speaking of flowers, not only do 90 different types of lilies exist, but no two of them are exactly alike.[7] All told, 369,000 different species of flowers are in the world.[8] If God makes sure the flowers have not only clothes to wear but exactly the right color, don't you think he will take care of you?

Practically speaking, how do you take the energy you waste on worry and invest it in something productive? The next verse tells us: "Seek first his kingdom and his righteousness, and all these things will be given to you as well" (verse 33).

What does it mean to seek first God's kingdom and his righteousness? It simply means you put God before everything else and anyone else, everywhere and all the time. Worry is when you're more concerned about anything than you are about God and his kingdom.

You see, if you seek first the kingdom of money, you'll worry about not only every dollar but every dime. If you seek first the kingdom of health, you'll worry about every skin spot and every headache. If you seek first the kingdom of popularity, you'll sweat every critical word somebody says about you. If you seek first the kingdom of safety, you'll be worried about every noise you hear at night.

A married couple was fast asleep one night when the wife shook her husband and said, "Get up. There's a burglar in the house!"

He sat up, but he didn't hear anything. "There's nobody in the house."

"I'm telling you there *is* somebody in the house. A burglar, and he's in the kitchen. Go see about it! And get the gun out of the drawer. You might need it."

He stumbled into the kitchen with the gun, and lo and behold, a burglar was ransacking the refrigerator. The homeowner raised his gun up and said, "Put your hands behind your back!"

Then when the man told the burglar to follow him, the thief said, "Are you taking me to the police?"

"No," the man answered, "I'm taking you to my bedroom."

"Why?"

"Because I want you to meet my wife."

"Why do you want me to meet her?"

"Because she's been worried about you for 33 years."

An all-powerful God says, *If you will make me your number one priority, seek my rule over you, surrender to me, and seek to be righteous before me, I'll take care of everything else.* In other words, he says, *If you take care of my business, I'll take care of yours.* That means putting today's worry in its proper position.

Remember that letter Ralph Waldo Emerson wrote to his daughter? Here's more of it:

> Finish each day and be done with it. You have done what you could. Some blunders, losses, and absurdities no doubt crept in; forget them as soon as you can. Tomorrow is a new day; let today go so you can begin tomorrow well and serenely, with too high a spirit to be encumbered with your old nonsense.[9]

And that leads us to putting tomorrow's worries in proper perspective.

## PUT TOMORROW'S WORRY IN PROPER PERSPECTIVE

Jesus covers tomorrow perfectly: "Do not worry about tomorrow, for tomorrow will worry about itself. Each day has enough trouble of its own" (Matthew 6:34).

God never promised he will give you strength for tomorrow, but he does give you strength for today, which has enough trouble of its own.

The word *worry* comes from the Old English word *wyrgan* from German, and it means "strangle."[10] That's a good word for it, because worry doesn't take the sorrow out of tomorrow; it just chokes the joy out of today. You can't change the past, but you can ruin a perfectly good present by worrying about the future. Mark Twain is thought to have said something along the lines of "I am an old man and have known a great many troubles, but most of them never happened."[11] The truth is the vast majorities of our worries are unnecessary. There's even a study that proves this.

The study looked into how many of the participants' imagined tragedies and fears never materialized. It turns out that 85 percent of things people worried about never happened. With the 15 percent that did happen, 79 percent of the people discovered either they could handle the problem better than they thought they could or the problem actually taught them a lesson worth learning. In other words, 97 percent of what we worry about is mainly our minds beating us up with things that either never happen or aren't nearly as bad as we thought they were.[12]

Most of the worries we manufacture should never leave the warehouse! A lady once received an email from a friend with an "urgent" tag on it. Here was the two-sentence message: "Start worrying now. I'll send details later."[13] Most of the time the details never arrive, or when they do, they amount to nothing serious.

I love the story about the third-grade schoolteacher who was introducing fractions to her class. They'd been working on learning how to multiply fractions, and she was quizzing them to see if they had grasped the concept. She couldn't help but laugh out loud when she asked a boy named William this question: "William, what is three-fourths of five-sixteenths?"

He replied, "I don't know exactly, but it isn't enough to worry about!"

Not exactly the right answer but a truly profound one!

More than that, worry is unfruitful. Jesus said in Matthew 6:27, "Can any one of you by worrying add a single hour to your life?" Worry doesn't change anything. It doesn't improve the situation. It never solved a problem, never lifted a burden, never answered a question, never dried a tear.

And here are two things you should never worry about: what you can change and what you can't change. If you can change it, do it, and if you can't, drop it. Do you understand the mathematics of worry? Worry *divides* the mind, *multiplies* misery, *subtracts* from happiness, and *adds* distress.

If you're ever going to get a handle on worry with the hands of faith, not the hands of fear, you've got to leave tomorrow alone. The calendar gives every day its own number because you're supposed to live them in the order God has arranged them. He hasn't called you to worry about tomorrow; he's simply called you to live for today. These words attributed to Robert D. Keppel are so wise: "Better never trouble trouble until trouble troubles you; for you only make your trouble double trouble when you do."

———

I've never seen a gravestone that read *He died of worry*. I've never seen a death certificate that said *Cause of death: worry.* Yet we've all heard of or known people who worried themselves to death. We now know that, medically and scientifically, that is possible. The bottom line of Jesus' whole sermon is simple: Worry is an insult to God. It's a slap in his face.

I was reading about how ocean liners are designed and learned that when the hull of a ship is pierced by means of some collision, the steel doors of the hull can be lowered so that only a portion of the ship is flooded. Let me make this application: When the ship of your life runs into the iceberg of trials, troubles, and tribulations unforeseen, lower the rear hold door of God's goodness against yesterday, lower the forward hold door of God's promises against tomorrow, and live safe and dry in the compartment of God's grace today.

A cross and an empty tomb tell us there's no problem God can't solve, there's no question God can't answer, and there's no situation God can't handle. The next time worry knocks at your door, let God answer it.

> All the water in the world,
> However hard it tried,
> Could never sink a ship
> Unless it got inside.
> All the hardships of this world
> Might wear you pretty thin,
> But they won't hurt you one least bit,
> Unless you let them in.[14]

You must put your worries where they belong, but every one of them is an opportunity to do what only you can do and trust God for what you can't do. If you take care of God's business, he'll take care of yours.

# ESCAPE THE JAIL CELL OF ANXIETY

*Nothing in the affairs of men is worthy of great anxiety.*

**PLATO**

One night when I was only a child, my wonderful, godly mother woke up, sat up in bed, and began to weep uncontrollably. As she slept, this thought had entered her mind: *There is no God, and you're going to hell.* For the next several months, doubt and despair stalked her at every turn. This was the first time she'd ever doubted the existence of God and worried that she would die and spend eternity in hell. A godly pastor helped pull her through over time, but what began as just a trickle of worry soon turned into a tsunami. She couldn't sleep. She began to lose her hair. She lost her appetite. She would walk the floor and have a panic attack.

Today her months-long ordeal would be called *generalized anxiety disorder* (GAD). According to the National Institute of Mental Health, GAD's characteristics include restlessness, fatigue, irritability, difficulty with sleeping, and overwhelming and uncontrollable feelings of worry.[1]

Here are some statistics to take in:

According to the Anxiety and Depression Association of America, "anxiety disorders are the most common mental illness in the U.S., affecting 40 million adults in the United States age 18 and older, or 18.1% of the population every year."[2]

By 2015, anxiety disorders in the United States were the "number one mental health problem among American women…second only to alcohol and drug abuse among men."[3]

And according to the World Health Organization (WHO), 1 in 13 [people] globally suffers from anxiety.[4]

According to an October 2020 public opinion poll released by the American Psychiatric Association, "62 percent of Americans felt more anxious" than they had a year before. That was, the report said, "a sizable increase over APA polls of the past three years, in which the number has ranged between 32% and 39%." The top causes of their anxiety were:

- Keeping themselves and their families safe (80%)

- COVID-19 (75%)

- Their health (73%)

- Gun violence (73%)

- The upcoming presidential election (72%)[5]

In his *The Anxiety & Phobia Workbook*, published in 2015, Edmund Bourne stated that researchers also speculated that the Western world's "environment and social order [had] changed more in the last thirty years than they [had] in the previous three hundred."[6] Just from a technology standpoint, think about it. Today we have the internet, smartphones, computer screens, televisions. We instantaneously hear any news about global warming, the threat of nuclear war, terrorist attacks, and the emergence of recently discovered deadly diseases. The intensity of our feelings have never been stronger, and anxiety has never been higher.

Here's my definition of anxiety: A lethal combination of worry and fear that dominates your mind, saturates your heart, and devastates your soul, which then continues to linger long after the actual threat or fear has dissipated. It has far greater intensity than just being worried. People use worry and anxiety interchangeably, but according to *Psychology Today*, "Worry tends to be more focused on thoughts in our heads, while anxiety is more visceral in that we feel it throughout our bodies."[7]

Even as I was writing this chapter, my 13-year-old grandson, who was spending the weekend with me, had my blood pressure kit out measuring his own blood pressure. He told me for the last three months he'd been having "anxiety attacks." When I asked him what they felt like, he said, "Pop, my chest hurts, and it feels as if I'm going to have a heart attack." He even told me he applies a soothing oil on his arm to calm him down.

It's important to note the differences between worry and anxiety.

- "Worry tends to reside in our minds. Anxiety affects both body and mind...

- Worry is specific. Anxiety is more generalized...

- Worry is ground in reality. Anxiety is marked by catastrophic thinking...

- Worry is temporary. Anxiety is longstanding...

- Worry doesn't impair function. Anxiety does."[8]

Here's the good news: The apostle Paul—with flesh and blood, sitting in a Roman prison, facing certain death, knowing he probably wouldn't get out of that prison alive and not knowing what day he would die—understood anxiety. In the book of the Bible called Philippians, he gives us a four-step process for how to escape the jail of anxiety. Both solid psychological advice and fantastic spiritual advice are found in Philippians 4:4-7. In just those three verses we're led to celebrate the person of the Lord, appreciate the presence of the Lord, liberate the power of the Lord, and meditate on the peace of the Lord.

## CELEBRATE THE PERSON OF THE LORD

What Paul first says about anxiety is so simple that it may sound simplistic at first. But let it sink in: "Do not be anxious about anything" (Philippians 4:6).

Yes, I know that's easy to say and hard to do. Everyone dealing with anxiety knows that in one sense you just can't turn anxiety on and off like water coming out of a spigot. On the other hand, two verses earlier, Paul confidently asserts that when anxiety attacks you, you attack anxiety. How? "Rejoice in the Lord always. I will say it again: Rejoice!" (Philippians 4:4).

Focus on his word *again*. Paul repeats himself to emphasize his point, so rejoicing in the Lord is not something you do only when you feel like it. You need to make rejoicing in the Lord—celebrating him—a habit. You need to build joy into the muscle memory of your heart, mind, and soul. Too many people wait until the anxiety alarm bells go off to focus on the Lord—on his goodness, on his grace, and on his greatness. By then, the wind of anxiety is so great that they snuff out that little matchstick of joy you tried to light.

You see, if you consistently rejoice in the Lord when things are good, when you're happy, then you'll be ready to rejoice in him when the clouds are thundering, the lightning is flashing, the wind is blowing, and the rain is pouring.

Paul also understood that it's hard to rejoice when pressures are great, problems are big, and people are mean. It's hard to rejoice when the walls are closing in and the roof is falling down and the foundation is coming apart. But he didn't say "rejoice in your circumstances."

For example, if you derive your joy from the stock market, your joy may crash. If you derive your joy from your marriage, your joy may die or divorce you. If you derive your joy from your business, your joy may declare bankruptcy. If you derive your joy from your children, your joy may move away or even turn away. If you derive your joy from your dream house, your joy may burn down or be foreclosed. But when you derive your joy from the Lord, your joy will never forsake you or fail you.

Are you under great pressure? The Lord is greater than that pressure. Do you have big problems? The Lord is bigger than your problems. Are you dealing with mean people? The Lord is stronger than those people. You won't find a lot of joy in possessions, popularity, or prosperity, but you can always rejoice in the greatness, the grace, and the goodness of the Lord.

In Dr. Earl Henslin's book titled *This Is Your Brain on Joy*, he wrote that joy and anxiety travel the same pathway in our brains, and it's normal for them to try to occupy the same path at the same time. That means we have to choose which one gets the right-of-way. He said if we open the gate for joy, anxiety has to get off the road; there's no room for both of them to come along.[9]

To deal with our anxiety, then, we should celebrate the person of the Lord.

## APPRECIATE THE PRESENCE OF THE LORD

Let's back up a step to verse 5, when Paul says, "Let your gentleness be evident to all. The Lord is near."

Gentleness is an attitude that's calm under fire and levelheaded. It doesn't overreact. It chooses faith over fear, trust over trembling, and worship over worry. It's the ability to keep your head when everybody else is losing theirs. Paul says it should be evident to everyone. But why?

When things that make you anxious come into your life, God is giving you an opportunity to show other people how a believer in God and a follower of Jesus responds. It's the chance for your family members, friends, coworkers, and neighbors to see how someone who truly believes that "God is with me and in control" reacts to the most difficult of situations. So when everyone else runs out, remain calm because God is right there with you. That calm is also contagious.

Those last four words Paul wrote are so huge because they tell us how we can maintain that gentleness—because "the Lord is near." Some scholars believe he was referring to the nearness of the second coming of the Lord, and that may be true. But I believe it also refers to the nearness of God in our lives and especially in our troubles. There is no need to fear when the Lord is near.

Too often we focus on the problems, the pressures, and the people causing our anxiety and forget about God. Instead, we should focus on God and let him handle the problems, the pressure, and the people causing our anxiety. Whatever is causing your anxiety, it's not meant to drive you into emotional despair and despondency; it's meant to drive you into the hands of an all-powerful God who already knows the answer to your question and the solution to your problem and can handle whatever you're facing.

Every time you pace the floor with your stomach in a knot and the ghost of anxiety is haunting every part of your home, you ought to say to yourself, *The Lord is near*. Knowing you can never get away from God and that God will never go away from you should bring tremendous comfort to you. No matter what foe you face, you're not fighting alone. No matter how hot the fire you're in, no matter how deep the pit you're in, the Lord is with you. You can't escape his presence.

## LIBERATE THE POWER OF THE LORD

Now let's get to the heart of the matter: "Do not be anxious about anything" (Philippians 4:6). The word *anxious* means "to be pulled apart" or "to divide."[10] That's exactly what happens psychologically, emotionally, and spiritually to anxious people. They feel like their lives are being pulled apart. They want to get a handle on the problem, but they can't seem to do it. They're hopeful but fearful.

The plant of anxiety often comes from the seed of worry, and anxiety is the monster that worry creates. But one French soldier wrote a prescription for this poisonous seed of worry that is just outstanding.

> Of two things one is certain. Either you are at the front of the lines or you are behind the lines. If you are at the front, one of two things is certain: either you are exposed to danger or you are in a safe place. If you are exposed to danger of two things one is certain: you are wounded or you are not wounded. If you are wounded of two things one is certain: you are either going to recover or you are going to die. If you recover there is no need to worry and if you die you can't worry.[11]

Now, overcoming anxiety is more than just an effort to quit worrying. With that, you probably wouldn't suffer from anxiety anyway. The key is being proactive to deal with it and know where to take it. This is Paul's advice: "In every situation, by prayer and petition, with thanksgiving, present your requests to God" (Philippians 4:6).

Be anxious about nothing and pray about everything. You know what we tend to do instead? We get anxious about everything and pray about nothing.

I love the joke about a man who went to see a doctor because both his ears were severely burned—almost black and crispy. The doctor looked at him and said, "This is horrible. How did you burn both of your ears?"

"Well, I didn't have any shirts to wear to a meeting, so I had to iron a shirt. I was hurrying because I was late, and when the phone rang, I was so stressed out and confused that I answered the iron instead of the phone."

"That's awful, but how did you burn the other ear?"

"The caller called again."

The truth is when you encounter pressures, and problems, and people, you'll either pick up the iron of anxiety or the phone of prayer.

Do you know what happens when you pray? You liberate the power of God. You get God involved. Prayer ignites the engine that allows the missile of God's power to blast off into your anxiety.

Permit me to use an example from my favorite football team, the Georgia Bulldogs. By common consensus, the greatest college running back of all time was Herschel Walker. He was a six-foot-one, 250-pound powerhouse who would leap over defensive lines in a single bound. Imagine you're a coach and you have one play left on the one-yard line, gunning for a national championship. Can you imagine leaving Herschel on the bench and running a pass-play to a brick-handed wide receiver? No, you'd give the ball to Herschel.

When we're filled with anxiety, too often we try to handle it ourselves. But we not only drop the ball; we never score. Prayer, however, brings your best player into the game, the One guaranteed to take you over the goal line every single time. When you try to handle anxiety yourself, it just deepens your anxiety. So when the avalanche of anxiety is coming down that mountain right on you, the tornado of trouble is tearing your soul, or the hurricane of heartache is pounding at the door of your heart, hear God's voice saying, *Give this to me. I've got it. Leave it to me and leave it with me.* He can handle it; you can't. He never said you could; he always said he would.

You can also be thankful that no matter how great the pressure, how difficult the people, or how hard the problem, God not only loves you enough to take them, but he's powerful enough to handle them and wise enough to grow you through them.

## MEDITATE ON THE PEACE OF THE LORD

When you follow those first three steps, here's what Paul says you can count on always happening: "The peace of God, which transcends all understanding, will guard your hearts and your minds in Christ Jesus" (Philippians 4:7).

A lot of peace treaties have been signed and then broken. The peace didn't last. God's peace does, but remember the peace of God is the peace that can come *only* from God. It's not the kind of peace you might find through drugs, alcohol, sex, fame, or fortune; that peace never lasts anyway. This is a peace that can't be bought, borrowed, or stolen. It's found in a deity—the one true God.

Eighteen of the New Testament books begin with a greeting of peace. But the peace we learn about from the Bible isn't from the authors of the books; it's from the God who inspired them to write the books. It's always grace first and then peace, because you can't know peace from God until you experience the grace of God. The word *peace* occurs nearly 400 times in the Bible, God's book of peace inspired by the God of peace. When you read the truth of God's Word and come to know the God who inspired it, you'll not only have peace but have a peace that transcends all understanding and will stand guard over your heart, soul, and mind 24 hours a day for as long as you live.

The steps are so simple yet so powerful. Imagine three boxes: one box is labeled *anxiety*, the second box is labeled *prayer*, and the third box is labeled *thanksgiving*. Now, in the anxiety box, put nothing. In the prayer box, put everything. In the thanksgiving box, put anything. Once you put things in the box where they belong, the peace and the assurance that God has everything under control will replace the anxiety you feel.

I want to remind you that final, real, lasting hope for overcoming your anxiety is the Lord. C.S. Lewis once explained, "God designed the human machine to run on Himself. He Himself is the fuel our spirits were designed to burn, or the food our spirits were designed to feed on…God cannot give us…a peace apart from Himself, because it is not there. There is no such thing."[12]

So let's review the four steps:

**C**elebrate the Person of the Lord

**A**ppreciate the Presence of the Lord

**L**iberate the Power of the Lord

**M**editate on the Peace of the Lord

The first letters spell *calm*. The next time your anxiety is up, let the Lord C A L M you down so that, like Paul, you can escape the jail cell of anxiety.

# ACCESS THE BRIDGE OVER TROUBLED WATERS

*Every man has his secret sorrows which the world knows not;*
*and often times we call a man cold when he is only sad.*

**HENRY WADSWORTH LONGFELLOW**

Some of the most listened-to songs of all time have been about feelings: "Hooked on a Feeling," "You've Lost That Loving Feeling," "Peaceful Easy Feeling." And now we'll deal with one of the most devastating feelings of all—depression.

Winston Churchill called it the black dog, and years ago, when I was living in Mississippi, it showed up at my house uninvited and unannounced. I went to bed on a Sunday night feeling great. Life was good. I was happy, the church I was pastoring was growing, my tennis game was in great shape, my marriage was strong, and I had beautiful sons. I was hitting on all eight cylinders.

Then when I woke up Monday morning, rolled over, and opened my eyes, that black dog was staring right at me. For the first time in my life I didn't want to get out of bed. I didn't want to talk to anybody. I didn't want to do anything. And I began the most difficult, darkest 90 days of my entire life. Every night the black dog slept by my bed, and every day he never left my side.

I still don't know why he showed up at my door, but I refer to that day as Black Monday because that was the day the stock market of my life completely crashed. I didn't know this dog's name at the time, but if you ever meet him, you'll know who he is.

Every day for three months, I went from being a pastor to an actor. I gave award-winning performances because I faked everything—smiles, laughter, and peace. It was a battle just to get out of bed in the morning. Every day felt like Halloween because I would put a mask on my face and pretend everything was fine. If you've ever been depressed, you know what I mean when I say that nothing is more depressing than being depressed.

In February of 2018, the *New York Times* ran an article about a psychology course being offered at Yale University. The course had become the most popular ever offered in the history of the school with nearly one fourth of Yale undergraduates enrolled in it. It was all about teaching students "how to lead a happier, more satisfying life." Perhaps that shouldn't be surprising. In 2013, "the Yale College Council found that more than half of undergraduates sought mental health care from the university during their time there."[1]

God's Word has a lot to say about our feelings and emotions. One of the things I love about Scripture is that when the Lord paints the portraits of biblical characters, they're not photoshopped. You see their warts and wrinkles. You see their flaws and faults. And now we're going to look at one of the most flawed men in the Bible—a prophet named Elijah.

## PORTRAIT OF A DEPRESSED MAN

If God had a Hall of Fame, Elijah would easily be elected on the first ballot. Filled with God's power, he was the first person in the Bible to raise a person from the dead, and his ministry is legendary. Yet as we're about to see, he was so depressed that he was suicidal. What's amazing is that he had every reason *not* to be depressed.

Before he fell into depression, Elijah was at the top of his game. He had just achieved one of the greatest single-handed victories in any battle or contest in history. He'd gone toe-to-toe with 450 false prophets of the pagan god Baal, and he'd defeated every one of them in a spiritual contest where everybody's life was on the line. And he was right and tight with God. Just before his depression, he'd predicted a nationwide drought that did come, and his prayers were so powerful that they not only caused God to stop the rain and cause the drought, but when he prayed again, God started the rain again and ended the drought.

Yet Elijah was depressed. Why? Because he was facing something that can make a man feel all kinds of emotion: the wrath of an angry woman.

Ahab was a wicked king who ruled over the nation of Israel, and his wife is one of the most infamous women in history. Her name was Jezebel, and she was a piece of work. (When was the last time you heard of a baby girl named Jezebel?) When word of what Elijah had done to Jezebel's prophets and that he was trying to turn the nation back to God got back to her, she hit the roof.

We read the story in 1 Kings: "Ahab told Jezebel everything Elijah had done and how he had killed all the prophets with the sword. So Jezebel sent a messenger to Elijah to say, 'May the gods deal with me, be it ever so severely, if by this time tomorrow I do not make your life like that of one of them'" (19:1-2).

Jezebel had put out a contract on Elijah's life, and in the blink of an eye he went from the mountaintop of delight to the valley of depression. But he managed to get out of that valley, and with God's help, so can you. Elijah found in God a bridge over the troubled waters of depression that's still available to us today. And to access that bridge, you must admit the reality of your depression, assess the reason for your depression, and apply the remedy of your depression.

## ADMIT THE REALITY
## OF YOUR DEPRESSION

It's important to understand that there's a difference between sadness and depression. It's natural for everyone to be sad sometimes. We all have those days when we're "down in the dumps" and have "the blues." Usually, sadness doesn't last long. But even if it lingers at times, you're still able to function, laugh, and live a normal life. But depression sticks with you like glue. Somebody put it this way: "Sadness is like a sprinter who eventually stops to rest. Depression is an endurance runner that just keeps going." When sadness becomes quicksand you can't get out of and blinds you from seeing the sunshine even on its brightest day, that's depression.

Here are some statistics:

- "Depression is the leading cause of disability in the United States among people ages 15-44."[2]

- "Depression ranks among the top 3 workplace issues in the United States, along with family crisis and stress."[3]

- "264 million people worldwide live with depression."[4]

No wonder depression has been called "the common cold of mental illness." Four degrees or stages of depression have been identified.

- *Dejection*—a temporary feeling of sadness

- *Discouragement*—a temporary feeling of hopelessness

- *Despondency*—an intense feeling of sadness that can last for weeks or months and affects eating habits and sleeping patterns

- *Despair*—a dangerous stage of emotional instability that can lead to thoughts of if not actual suicide[5]

If you're at any of these four stages, particularly the last one, start by admitting it to somebody. Don't hold it in. Unfortunately, that's what Elijah did: "He himself went a day's journey into the wilderness. He came to a broom bush, sat down under it and prayed that he might die. 'I have had enough, Lord,' he said. 'Take my life; I am no better than my ancestors'" (1 Kings 19:4).

Elijah was honest enough to let the Lord and anyone within earshot know he was depressed. There's no shame in admitting it. Good people, godly people, and great people get depressed. Kings, prophets, prime ministers, CEOs, and, yes, pastors get depressed.

Abraham Lincoln got so depressed he said, "I am now the most miserable man living. If what I feel were equally distributed to the whole human family, there would not be one cheerful face on earth...To remain as I am is impossible; I must die or get better."[6]

Be courageous enough to admit the reality of depression.

## ASSESS THE REASON
## FOR YOUR DEPRESSION

It's not always possible to pinpoint one particular cause of depression, but sometimes why someone is depressed is obvious. If you're depressed, you need to stop and consider your situation.

One of the amazing things about depression is that it will often attack you not because life is going poorly but just when life is going well. Elijah has just come off of a great victory when he went toe-to-toe with those 450 false prophets and defeated them and destroyed their false ministry. Now he's gone from his highest high to his lowest low. It happens often. That's why a football team can win a big game against a tough opponent and then get squashed the next week. Christmas is my favorite time of the year. Do you know what my least favorite time of the year is? The week after Christmas. Easter is normally the highest high a pastor will ever experience, but you don't even want to know what the Monday after Easter is like.

Here's a warning: If you're depressed, you'll be tempted to hibernate in isolation. But that's the worst possible choice. Elijah committed the cardinal error, the fatal mistake when dealing with depression: He totally isolated himself and got away from anybody who could help him. When you're depressed, you'll be tempted to withdraw—to go to bed, pull the covers over yourself, and wallow in your own self-pity. People rarely ever commit suicide in front of anyone else. They do it alone.

In my research on depression, I discovered at least three triggers for it.

## Physical Triggers

Sometimes depression can be physically triggered. Elijah had basically run the equivalent of 12 marathons. He'd run the length of Israel all the way down to Beersheba, which is where the border for Israel ended—a distance of 300 miles. He'd also just come off of a long fast. His strength was gone. He was hungry, thirsty, and physically exhausted.

If you're a workaholic working late at night, rising early, eating junk food on the go, and skipping exercise, then you're a prime candidate for depression. If you're a stay-at-home parent caring for crying children with unending household duties, you're a prime candidate for depression. We now know depression can also be caused by chemical imbalances in the brain. The brain has chemical messengers called neurotransmitters. When those transmitters are healthy and normal, we are too. When those transmitters are absent, it can trigger major depression. This is why some people may need medication to regulate these chemicals.

## Emotional Triggers

Sometimes depression can be emotionally triggered. Some people experience what I call "4-D" depression, caused by death, disease, divorce, or disaster. The majority of depressed people I've dealt with have depression that can usually be traced to one of those four things—for example, the death of a loved one, a life-threatening disease, divorce, or the loss of a job. Any of these can cause emotions to come crashing down like an avalanche.

## Spiritual Triggers

We must never discount that depression can be spiritually triggered. If you're living in unconfessed, unrepented sin, then divinely sent depression is probably knocking at your door. Of course, God doesn't want you depressed. The problem is that other spiritual forces at work in this world do. I believe in a literal devil, and I believe Satan is the ultimate joy-killer.

Do you know what psychologists say they've discovered is close to if not the number one cause of depression? Repressed anger or what we call bitterness. When people become bitter at others or even God and then internalize it, the milk of bitterness curdles into depression. (We'll talk about bitterness in chapter 9.)

Now, if you really can't pinpoint the reason for your depression, don't let that depress you. You can activate a potential cure even if you don't know the actual cause.

## APPLY THE REMEDY
## FOR YOUR DEPRESSION

There's nothing wrong with being depressed, but one should always seek ways to keep from staying depressed. There are indications that every person in the Bible who was depressed and managed their depression overcame it. Now, you may still need professional help, and you may need to see a health care professional to see if you have a medical issue, but you can take these three steps on your own to deal with depression. They're right in our 1 Kings text.

### 1. Physically recharge.

Notice what Elijah does next:

> Then he lay down under the bush and fell asleep. All at once an angel touched him and said, "Get up and eat." He looked around, and there by his head was some bread baked over hot coals, and a jar of water. He ate and drank and then lay down again. The angel of the LORD came back a second time and touched him and said, "Get up and eat, for the journey is too much for you." So he got up and ate and drank. Strengthened by that food, he traveled forty days and forty nights until he reached Horeb, the mountain of God (1 Kings 19:5-8).

Elijah did some things that immediately helped his mood. First, he took a nap, got some sleep and much-needed rest, and ate. When you're depressed, do you often find it hard to sleep and eat? That just makes matters worse. One of the most spiritual things you can do sometimes is just take a break—take a nap, relax, rest, and eat a good meal. Never underestimate some good old-fashioned R and R to recover your emotional equilibrium.

## 2. *Spiritually refresh.*

When you get depressed, you'll be tempted to obsess over your problems. That was one of the biggest mistakes Elijah made. When he started looking down and around instead of looking up and above, he was overwhelmed: "'I have had enough, LORD,' he said. 'Take my life; I am no better than my ancestors'" (1 Kings 19:4).

Elijah had completely lost sight of God and who he was before God. He was attending the one party you should never ever go to—a pity party. God doesn't do pity parties. He will have compassion on you, but he won't enter into a pity party with you. Besides, who told Elijah he was no better than his ancestors? And who told him he had to be? Nobody.

Then God steps in and changes his entire focus.

> The LORD said, "Go out and stand on the mountain in the presence of the LORD, for the LORD is about to pass by." Then a great and powerful wind tore the mountains apart and shattered the rocks before the LORD, but the LORD was not in the wind. After the wind there was an earthquake, but the LORD was not in the earthquake. After the earthquake came a fire, but the LORD was not in the fire. And after the fire came a gentle whisper (verses 11-12).

When Elijah quit looking down and started looking up, when he quit thinking about himself and started thinking about God, everything changed. What specifically did Elijah do? He listened for God to speak. If God has your ear, he will speak to you. If God has your heart, he will minister to you. I can't emphasize enough to you that when you're depressed, you can't do anything more important than get into God's Word and listen to his voice.

One of the things that helped me get through my period of depression was that every single day I did the one thing I'd always done every single day—I got into God's Word, calmed my spirit, and listened for the voice of God. No, he never spoke out loud, but he always spoke softly and clearly. You know that's normally the way God speaks.

When an eardrum detects vibrations caused by soundwaves, we hear. The intensity of those waves is measured in decibels. Air-horns sound at 110 decibels, thunderclaps at 120 decibels, and jackhammers at 100 decibels. Jet engines sound at 150 decibels.[7] It's important to know that "above 140 [decibels], sounds cause humans physical distress: shortness of breath, nausea, nosebleeds, and other severe discomforts. Below that level, they can still cause permanent problems, including hearing loss and persistent tinnitus." And you can actually be killed by soundwaves above 200 decibels.[8]

What's on the other end of the sound spectrum, measuring in at just 20 decibels? A whisper![9] I cannot tell you how many times I've read my Bible in complete silence and heard God whisper through his Word. Do you want to know another reason I believe God speaks in whispers? Because to hear a whisper, you've got to get close to someone and put your ear right next to their mouth. If you lean into God to hear his whisper, that's exactly what he wants. Nothing refreshes you spiritually like listening to God's Word.

## 3. *Socially reengage.*

Notice what the master psychologist says to Elijah: "The LORD said to him, 'Go back the way you came, and go to the Desert of Damascus. When you get there, anoint Hazael king over Aram. Also, anoint Jehu son of Nimshi king over Israel, and anoint Elisha son of Shaphat from Abel Meholah to succeed you as prophet'" (1 Kings 19:15-16).

Isolation is a shovel that only digs the hole of depression deeper. God tells Elijah to get out of his pity party, get out of his isolation cage, and go out and minister to other people. One of the greatest psychiatrists of the twentieth century was Dr. Karl Menninger. We're told someone asked for his best piece of advice for a person going through mental distress. He said, "Lock up your house...find someone in need and do something for him."[10]

———

Jesus Christ knew what it was to go through the darkest depths of the soul. But at the bottom of his own valley, he climbed up a hill and died on a cross. Then God raised him from the valley of death to the mountain of resurrection. If God can raise his Son from the dead, he can raise your soul from the deep. If Jesus can turn water into wine, he can turn your depression into joy. *He* is the bridge over troubled waters.

# PLACE YOUR FAITH IN THE ONE AND ONLY

*I learned that courage was not the absence of fear, but the triumph over it. The brave man is not he who does not feel afraid, but he who conquers that fear.*

**NELSON MANDELA**

Fear—we all know what it is. It's one of the most debilitating emotions known to the human race. Fear is unbelievably powerful. It penetrates the heart, it poisons the spirit, and it paralyzes the soul.

The late, great trumpet player Louis Armstrong told a story about when he was a boy in Louisiana and an old woman asked him to get her a bucket of water:

> I went down to the spring…and I started to dip the bucket when I saw a pair of mean ol' eyes looking up at me from the water. I jumped up and went running back. That old woman stared at me and said, "Louie, where's my bucket of water?" and I said, "Miss Hallie Mae, I can't get you any water. There's a big ol' alligator in that spring!"

And she said, "Louis, that alligator's been there for years. That critter is just as scared of you as you are of him."

And I said, "Miss Hallie Mae, if that alligator is as afraid of me as I am of him, believe me, that water ain't fit to drink!"[1]

We have seen the power of fear firsthand. It can cause banks to fold, make money go into hiding, and turn stocks into rocks and Dow Jones into bare bones. Individually, it can affect you physically, mentally, and emotionally. A panic attack can make you break out into a sweat, tie your stomach into knots, shove a lump into your throat, and shut down your entire windpipe. It can cause your blood pressure to rise like a rocket and your courage to drop like a rock.

In fact, if you suddenly become afraid of something quickly and strongly enough, the blood can be cut off almost completely from the brain and cause you to faint. It can also cause the blood flow to the extremities of the body to be hindered so quickly that you actually "get cold feet."

Fear can even kill you. Medical science has proven it can cause the cardiovascular muscles to react in such a way that heart failure is the result, meaning that people can literally be "scared to death." Fear can cause you to do things that you otherwise wouldn't normally do and keep you from doing things you know you should do.

The fact is we often fear the wrong things, and many of our fears are irrational or unnecessary. In his book *Put Your Dream to the Test*, John Maxwell tells us "fear often has no connection to reality." He lists several examples.

- Airports sell catastrophic life insurance, yet "people are more likely to choke on food than to die on a commercial aircraft."

- People "fear being stabbed to death by a stranger, yet they are twice as likely to be killed playing a sport."

- People "fear being killed by a shark, yet barnyard pigs kill more people than sharks do."

- People "fear dying during a medical procedure, yet they are sixteen times more likely to die in a car accident than from a medical complication."[2]

As a boy—even into my teenage years—I refused to get into an elevator alone for fear of its falling. Yet the chance of dying in an elevator is "about one in 10.5 million, which is a .0000000958% chance."[3] Elevators are even safer than taking the stairs![4]

Franklin D. Roosevelt gave one of the most famous quotes in presidential history when he said, "The only thing we have to fear is...fear itself." That sounds good, but it's simply not true. Come face-to-face with a scorpion, a spider, a rattlesnake, or a terrorist and simply say, "The only thing I have to fear is fear itself" and see how far that gets you!

There is a good kind of fear. It's called the "fear of God." Proverbs 1:7 reminds us that "the fear of the LORD is the beginning of knowledge" (ESV). And in some cases, fear isn't necessarily a bad thing. In fact, Jesus even taught us to fear. He said in Matthew 10:28, "Fear him who can destroy both soul and body in hell" (ESV). I think you know who he meant—Satan.

But there's a bad kind of fear that's never from God and never leads to God but rather leads away from God: the spirit of fear. In just one sentence in a letter he wrote to a young protégé named Timothy, Paul shows us how we can put our fears in proper perspective. We need to realize that "For God gave us a spirit not of fear but of power and love and self-control" (2 Timothy 1:7 ESV).

If we allow ourselves to be controlled by a spirit of fear as followers of Christ, that spirit will starve our faith and feed our doubt. It will force us to run when we should stand, and it will force us to be quiet when we should speak up. We should fight this fear, and here's how you can do it: admit your fear, activate your faith, and acknowledge the Father.

## ADMIT YOUR FEAR

Everybody at one time or another deals with the spirit of fear. The primary word for "fear" in the New Testament is the Greek word *phobos*. We get the word *phobia* from that. Did you know that psychiatrists and doctors have identified more than 700 different kinds of phobias? Here are just five:

- *Acrophobia* is the fear of high places.

- *Claustrophobia* is the fear of enclosed places.

- *Ergophobia* is the fear of work.

- *Demophobia* is the fear of crowds.

- *Pentheraphobia* is the fear of mothers-in-law. (Leaner [my nickname for my mother-in-law], I don't have that fear of you. For the record, I have only love!)

Even though you may not struggle with phobias, we all struggle with fears. The first step to overcoming whatever fear you have is to admit it but also to analyze it and put it in its proper perspective. Fear is nothing to be ashamed of, and the truth is everybody is affected by it.

You can walk with God, be super spiritual, read your Bible, and pray yet still have to battle fear. I do. God knows that about us. That's why he has to tell us—his own family, his own children—not to fear 365 times in the Bible.

You need to understand how fear works. First, it gets into your mind, and then you begin to dwell on it. Then it gets into your heart, and then you begin to live with it. Then it begins to dominate your will, and then it becomes the engine that drives everything in your life. If you're not careful, you'll let fear paralyze you, neutralize you, and monopolize you.

Some of you need to be liberated from the shackles of fear that are strangling your heart, your soul, and even your life.

Next you need to activate your faith.

## ACTIVATE YOUR FAITH

God has given a foolproof, fail-safe key that could unlock the iron gates of fear and free you from its prison forever. But only one key fits—faith.

I want to show you what I call the Faith Index. This is how fear and faith operate. When fear increases, faith decreases. When faith increases, fear decreases.

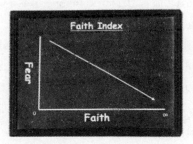

When you think about it, fear is simply the absence of faith. You never fear anything you believe you can handle or believe somebody else can handle for you. The only time you fear something is when you believe you can't handle it or that no one can handle it for you. That's where God comes in!

If you knew you had within you the power to face anything that comes into your life and handle it—knowing that no matter what it may do to you, it can never keep you from God's love nor God's plan for your life—then you would never fear anything.

Well, as a follower of Jesus, you have the power of God's Spirit in you! There's no foe you can't face. There's no fight you can't win. There's no fear you can't conquer if God's power is within you. First John 4:4 says, "He who is in you is greater than he who is in the world" (ESV).

God is in you! God is for you! God is with you! If God brings you to it, God will bring you through it. But there's more: "For God gave us a spirit not of fear but of power and *love*" (2 Timothy 1:7 ESV, emphasis mine). We not only have the power of God to fight our fears but the love of God to face our fears. Three words ought to put fear where it belongs in your life, for the rest of your life: *God loves me.*

As the verse continues, we see that God has given us one other thing to help us in this battle against fear: "For God gave us a spirit not of fear but of power and love and *self-control*" (emphasis mine). What does Paul mean by self-control? It means "a sound mind." God has given us the ability to discern and understand what fear is and what fear can do and what fear cannot do.

We've learned that so much of fear is unfounded and ungrounded. A University of Michigan study determined that 60 percent of our fears are totally unwarranted, and 20 percent have already become past activities and are completely out of our control. Another 10 percent are so petty they don't make any difference and of the remaining 10 percent, and only 4 to 5 percent are real and justifiable. Half of those we can't do anything about, so they concluded only 2 percent of our fears are real to begin with.[5]

But what about that 2 percent? Now, that's where faith must kick in.

David of the Bible was captured by the Philistines once, and he thought for sure he would be executed. He was scared, and this was indeed a valid fear. Do you know what he said? "When I am afraid, I put my trust in you" (Psalm 56:3). David understood that the answer to fear is faith.

You have to come to the point when you say, *God, no matter what happens to me, no matter if things don't work out the way I want them to, even if it costs me my life, I will trust you.*

These words are famously carved above a fireplace mantel in a hotel in England: "Fear knocked at the door. Faith answered. No one was there."[6] Remember, the higher the faith, the lower the fear. You may be asking, *How do you activate your faith when you're absolutely scared out of your mind? How do you decrease the fear factor and increase the faith factor? How do you make the fear index go down and the faith index go up?*

You acknowledge the Father.

## ACKNOWLEDGE THE FATHER

The first two words of 2 Timothy 1:7 are the most important: "For God." When you bring God into the picture, why should fear have any place in the portrait? The great preacher Charles Spurgeon said, "If you know Jesus Christ as your Lord you don't need to fear the past. It has been forgiven. You don't need to fear the present. God will provide. You don't need to fear the future, because your eternal destiny is secure."[7]

Let me bring this full circle. The way to decrease your fear is to increase your faith. The way to increase your faith is to change your focus. When you focus on your fear, faith goes down and fear goes up. When you focus on the Father, faith goes up and fear goes down.

———

Many of us remember September 11, 2001, recalling the fear and chaos surrounding the attack on the Twin Towers in New York City. In our minds, we can still see people running from the towers in pursuit of safety and the horror and fear on their faces. Then the strong and sturdy towers came crashing down in a thunderous roar that could be heard miles away.

With that in mind, think of Proverbs 18:10: "The name of the LORD is a strong tower; the righteous runs into it and is safe" (NASB). God is an unfailing tower of power, of love, and of a sound mind who can handle anything that comes your way. So fear not! Fear not! Fear not! We serve a God who holds the whole world in his hands, and that includes you and me. He has not, he cannot, he will not fail! So put your faith in the One and only—your heavenly Father.

# REACH UP AND REACH OUT

*Loneliness, far from being a rare and curious phenomenon...*
*is the central and inevitable fact of human existence.*

**THOMAS WOLFE**

Each year more than four million tourists visit Yellowstone National Park. Its numerous attractions spread across the 2.2-million-acre park, but only the most adventurous tourists and veteran hikers attempt to visit one particular place.

Thorofare Ranger Station is hidden deep in the southeastern corner of the park and is considered the most remote place in the continental United States.[1] In fact, it's more than 20 miles from the nearest road. And if you're a ranger assigned to this station, you will drive about 15 miles from the park, then get on horseback and travel 32 miles into the wilderness, which is the shortest route.

If you're a serious hiker, this excursion might be on your bucket list. But why? The area is filled with dangerous animals, including grizzly bears and wolverines. From the sky, it's just a dark spot on a map. There are no lights. It's a place where time is measured only by moons and seasons.[2] So what is it about this place that's so attractive to hikers? Why would anyone want to go there? Because it's one of the few places in nature where someone can be truly alone.

I think an even more remote place is the heart of a lonely person. Lonely people are everywhere, and they have few external characteristics. Some have downturned faces or sad eyes, but most simply blend in with the world around them. You could be living next to someone you have no idea is lonely. Or maybe you're one of the unnoticed lonely people.

In a 2020 survey by the health insurer Cigna, three in five Americans said they were lonely, a 7 percentage-point increase from 2018. And social media users were "significantly more likely to feel alone, isolated, left out and without companionship."[3] Loneliness is on the rise.

People from all walks of life experience loneliness. Prosperity can't insure against it, position can't rise above it, and power can't stand before it. Can anybody, anywhere, at any time, at any place be more miserable than someone who feels they have no one who cares about them, loves them, or looks after them?

In 2013 construction workers in Rotterdam, Netherlands, went to a 74-year-old woman's apartment to replace her gas pipes. When she repeatedly failed to respond to her doorbell, they called the police, who found a pile of the woman's mail inside the door. Then they found her decayed corpse. With some of the mail ten years old, they realized that was how long she'd been dead.[4] How lonely she must have been.

A 2019 Life Health Network article that related that story also said, "Recently, *The New York Times* featured a study on loneliness and deemed our society as experiencing a 'loneliness epidemic.'" In fact, the article went on to say, "Loneliness and weak social connections are associated with a reduced lifespan similar to someone smoking fifteen cigarettes a day and are associated with having a greater risk of reduced lifespan than someone with obesity."[5] In January 2019, Dr. Vivek Murthy, who at this writing is the U.S. Surgeon General for a second time, stated, "During my years caring for patients, the most common pathology I saw was not heart disease or diabetes…It was loneliness."[6]

Also in January 2019, the U.S. Health Resources & Services Administration said, "Two in five Americans report that they sometimes or always feel their social relationships are not meaningful, and one in five say they feel lonely or socially isolated." They also reported that Brigham Young University professor and psychologist Julianne Holt-Lunstad, who in April 2017 testified before the U.S. Senate, said "the lack of connection can have life threatening consequences" and "that the problem is structural as well as psychological."

The report further said that "the average household size in the U.S. has declined in the past decade, leading to a 10 percent increase in people living alone. According to the U.S. Census Bureau, over a quarter of the U.S. population—and 28 percent of older adults—now live by themselves."[7]

And here's more information from that report: One in six baby boomers (those born 1946 to 1964) lived alone, one out of two people felt lonely (and so *are* lonely), and millennials (those born in the 1980s or 1990s) and Generation Z (those born in the late 1990s and early 2000s) had the highest rates of loneliness.[8]

In a Loma Linda University Health article from May 2020, Carolina Osorio, MD, a geriatric psychiatrist at Loma Linda Behavioral Health Institute, is quoted speaking about the effects of social distancing during the COVID-19 pandemic: "The research tells us those lonely people are more likely to become ill, experience cognitive decline and die earlier than those with more social lives."[9]And again in the 2019 U.S. Health Resources & Services Administration report, we're told that "an estimated $6.7 billion in annual federal spending is attributable to social isolation among older adults. Poor social relationships were associated with a 29 percent increase in risk of coronary heart disease and a 32 percent rise in the risk of stroke."[10]

If you battle loneliness, you're in company with the man who wrote Psalm 102. Imagine you're his counselor and you hear him say, "I am like a desert owl, like an owl among the ruins. I lie awake; I have become like a bird alone on a roof" (verses 6-7).

What was his problem? Loneliness. He felt like an isolated owl that wonders if anyone gives a hoot. Hearing those words, many of you may be thinking, *That's exactly how I feel.* If it is, I have good news. There's a way up and out of your loneliness. Let's find it together.

## LET'S SEE THE PROBLEM OF LONELINESS

Now, there's a big difference between being alone and being lonely. You can be alone without being lonely. Some people are loners. They don't mind being alone and don't feel lonely when they are alone. Sometimes we all need to be alone.

You can also be lonely without being alone. As I related in another book, "You can be in a crowd of thousands of people and still feel lonely. Henry David Thoreau once said, 'A city is a place where hundreds of people are lonely together.'"[11]

When I moved from Georgia to Florida to attend college, I was suddenly eating with, going to class with, and interacting with scores of people every day. But I had never been as lonely in my life, and I was miserable in my loneliness. I grew to understand that loneliness is not just lonesomeness. Loneliness is not isolation in space; it's insulation in spirit. It's the feeling that you're cut off, unnoticed, unloved, uncared for, unneeded—and maybe even unnecessary.

The silence of loneliness is deafening. You can hear it...

- At night as you crawl into a bed that's half empty because your spouse has left you or passed away.

- In a home that's quiet because all the kids have moved out and you realize why an "empty nest" can be sad.

- In an empty mailbox at Christmas or on your birthday.

- In a computer because your email in-box dries up.

- In a phone that never rings because no one seems to call anymore.[12]

There's no feeling quite like it, because we all want to be noticed, thought about, and cared for by somebody. In his book *Pleasing God*, R.C. Sproul wrote,

> Sigmund Freud once told the story of a schoolboy who was expelled from school for misbehavior. He stood outside the classroom and threw pebbles against the windows.
>
> Finally the principal went outside and confronted the boy. "Why are you throwing rocks against the windows?"
>
> "Because I just wanted everyone to know that I'm still here."[13]

So many of us still carry rocks in our pockets. We want people to know we're "still here."

The reason we despise loneliness is that it's so destructive. It can do untold damage to the psyche and to the mind. In 2018, two psychologists wrote for the Australian Psychological Society that "most [general practitioner physicians] struggle with 'frequent attenders.' While this group represents just 10 percent of all patients, they take up as many as 50 percent of appointments. Frequent attenders typically have complex and chronic health problems—and often both physical and mental health conditions."[14]

One of the major causes of suicide is the overwhelming feeling of loneliness, but loneliness increases the risk of premature death from every cause—and for every race. Among black people, for instance, loneliness doubles the risk of early death, and in white people it increases the risk between 60 to 84 percent.[15] Loneliness is associated with a 40 percent increase in a person's risk of dementia.[16]

We must see the problem of loneliness.

## LET'S STATE THE PRESENCE OF LONELINESS

To battle the problem of loneliness successfully, you have to at least understand why you're lonely. There's simply no denying the existence or the effects of loneliness. Have you ever noticed that people never drink alone in TV beer commercials? They're always drinking with someone else. The subliminal message is that you won't be lonely in places like a bar. Loneliness, however, can be a feeling of helplessness that no matter what you do or where you go or who you're with, you are and forever will be lonely.

One summer evening a violent thunderstorm was overhead as a mother tucked her little boy into bed. She was about to turn off the light when, with a tremble in his voice, her son said, "Mommy, will you sleep with me tonight?"

The mother smiled and gave him a reassuring hug. "Honey, I can't do that. I have to sleep with your daddy."

He looked up at her and said, "The big baby."

Did you know there are different kinds of loneliness? Sometimes loneliness is just an infrequent state that will pass, and other times it becomes one's experience of life. Dr. Jeffrey Young of Columbia University describes three kinds of loneliness: transient, situational, and chronic.

*Transient loneliness* lasts anywhere from a few minutes to a few hours, and periodically almost everyone experiences this kind of loneliness.

Then there is *situational loneliness* that results from a significant event. You're lonely because your spouse dies, your best friend moves away, or you move to a totally different location where you don't know anyone.

The worst loneliness of all is *chronic loneliness*. This is when people tend to become preoccupied with themselves and with their problems. In effect, they determine to be lonely. Dr. Young classifies as chronically lonely individuals people who feel lonely for more than two years at a time apart from any traumatic event.[17]

Many people are lonely because they want to be lonely. Some of them will tell you they are just "loners," and for others it may be due to a fear of intimacy or depth or potential heartache. Maybe due to a wound in their past, they self-isolate and insulate in order to feel safe. Regardless, they are alone because they choose to be.

I personally believe that one of the greatest causes of loneliness is a lack of a true, real, intimate relationship with God. Have you ever considered that one of the first human emotions Adam felt in the garden of Eden was loneliness? After his sin, there was a wedge between him and Eve and his fellowship with God had been cut off. There's no greater loneliness than when you feel cut off from not only people but also from the God who wants to live in you.

So take stock right now if you're battling loneliness and ask yourself why you're lonely. Then assess whether—with God's help—you can correct, change, or manage whatever is causing you to be lonely.

This leads to the most important thing we need to address.

# LET'S STOP THE
# POWER OF LONELINESS

Loneliness is a void that needs to be filled, and lonely people want to fill it. They might even go to great lengths to do it. One man went to see a psychiatrist and asked him if he could give him a split personality.

The doctor said, "Why do you want a split personality?"

"Because that way I would have somebody to talk to."

You don't need a split personality to take care of loneliness, but let me tell you about two things you can do—reach up and reach out.

## Reach Up

Jesus understands your loneliness. Did you know that Psalm 102, the psalm that says in verse 6, "I am like a desert owl," is what is called a Messianic psalm? That means it's a prophecy of Jesus. This psalmist is talking about what Jesus experienced, about what he felt. In fact, as mentioned in the introduction to this book, there was a moment on the cross when Jesus Christ experienced the ultimate loneliness that no human being has ever experienced.

Listen to the following verses from Psalm 102: "All day long my enemies taunt me; those who rail against me use my name as a curse. For I eat ashes as my food and mingle my drink with tears because of your great wrath, for you have taken me up and thrown me aside" (verses 8-10).

Again, do you remember what Jesus said at his greatest point of agony on the cross? "My God, my God, why have you forsaken me?" (Matthew 27:46). He experienced the ultimate loneliness when his own Father, the God who had loved him from eternity past to eternity future, turned his back. Jesus Christ was the loneliest person who has ever lived or will ever live.

That's why I can tell you that, if you're a child of God, you're not lonely because you're alone. You enjoy the permanent company of God the Father, who said, "Never will I leave you; never will I forsake you" (Hebrews 13:5). God the Father will not turn his back on you. God the Son will not turn his back on you. God the Holy Spirit will not turn his back on you. You can always talk to Jesus. You can always enjoy the presence of Jesus. You can always share with him your loneliness, because he knows what it is to be alone, and he knows what it is to be lonely.

You enjoy unbroken fellowship with God the Son who said, "Surely I am with you always" (Matthew 28:20). And you enjoy the continuing presence of God the Holy Spirit, whom Jesus said will be "with you forever" (John 14:16).

### Reach Out

My first piece of advice to you was to *reach up* to the Lord. Now I say to *reach out*. Reach out to someone who's hurting worse than you are, who may be lonelier than you are. Befriend them and be a blessing to them. Have you ever considered that when you minister to someone else who's lonely, then two people have their loneliness cured—you and that other person?

———

These wise words are from a character in a novel, through the pen of the story's author: "It is nothing new to be lonely. It comes to all of us sooner or later...If we try to retreat from it, we end in a darker hell... But if we face it, if we remember that there are a million others like us, if we try to reach out to comfort them and not ourselves, we find in the end that we are lonely no longer."[18]

A number of years ago I met a woman named Alma, who told me she became pregnant in 1939. She was just 16 years old, she wasn't married, and in that day it was a public shame to be a so-called "unwed mother." She was deserted by all of her former friends, and when much of her family even turned their back on her, she was a social outcast. She felt so alone. She said, "Loneliness was killing me."

She admitted that she was contemplating suicide one day when she suddenly heard, *Alma, you are not alone if you have me.* That's all the voice kept saying: *Alma, you are not alone if you have me.* And at that point she began to honestly and diligently seek the Lord. She got on her knees and asked Jesus Christ to come into her heart.

Alma then looked at me and said something I will never forget: "Pastor Merritt, that was over 50 years ago, and today I still know that as long as I have Jesus, I am never alone." That beautiful lady was right.

No one in this life is so wise, so strong, or so powerful that they can guarantee you will never experience the feeling that you're completely alone. But facts are more important than feelings. The fact is the moment you come to know God through his Son, Jesus Christ, you will never be alone again.

# SLAY THE GREEN-EYED MONSTER

*It is not love that is blind, but jealousy.*

**LAWRENCE DURRELL,** *JUSTINE*

Channelview, Texas, is a quiet middle-class suburb of Houston, made up of nice homes, nice cars, and nice families. But years ago this entire community was turned upside down by a story that's still hard to believe, and it all stemmed from a cheerleading competition.

Amber and Shanna lived right around the corner from each other and had been friends for years. Their mothers were close friends, and the girls were classmates at the same private Christian school. Amber was president of the Student Council, and Shanna was vice president. The moms even took turns carpooling the kids to school.

Everything seemed fine between these families for years—until the girls were in sixth grade. That's when Amber beat out Shanna for a cheerleading spot.

The two girls had always competed against each other, but Amber had been competing in beauty contests since she was four, and she always seemed to have the edge over Shanna. Shanna's mother, who attended a local Christian church, began to resent Amber for always beating out her daughter. She even tried unsuccessfully to get Amber disqualified from the cheerleading competition by invoking a technicality in the rules. One year she showed up at school on the day students voted for cheerleader candidates and handed out rulers and pencils with a campaign slogan: "Shanna for Cheerleader." As a result of her mother's actions, Shanna was disqualified.

Finally, it all hit a boiling point for Shanna's mother. She felt she couldn't live like that any longer, and she decided to hire a hitman to kill Amber and her mother. While she was looking for a suitable contract killer, she mentioned her plan to her former brother-in-law, who notified the police. An undercover cop wearing a wire posed as a hitman and connected with Shanna's mother. According to tape recordings, he told her he would kill the mother for $5,000 and the daughter for $2,500.

Shanna's mother couldn't come up with that much cash, so she gave the "hitman" a pair of diamond earrings as a down payment for killing just the mother. She was arrested for solicitation of capital murder and sentenced to 15 years in jail, though she was released 6 months later due to a technicality.[1]

What made this mother into a monster? But in fact, she wasn't a monster. She was made in the image of God, just like the rest of us. But she also had a sin nature, just like the rest of us. Then she was afflicted by the green-eyed monster called "jealousy."

Jealousy is somewhat like a fire in a closed grill—it is burning hot but no one can see it though others may "feel the heat." You may look cool on the outside, but jealousy can heat up the furnace of your heart to a thousand degrees. And when it finally boils over, it can wreak havoc.

We've been dealing with one of the most powerful driving forces in all of our lives—our emotions. Now we're dealing with one of the most destructive of emotions: jealousy. The wisest man who ever lived—Solomon of the Bible—said this about it: "Anger is cruel and fury overwhelming, but who can stand before jealousy?" (Proverbs 27:4).

Perhaps you've read how the Pharisees made sure Jesus was crucified, but do you know what their primary motive was? Matthew 27:18 says, "Pilate knew that it was because of jealousy that the chief priests and elders had handed Jesus over to him" (Matthew 27:18 AMP). In one sense, then, we can say that jealousy killed Jesus. The green-eyed monster drove the nails through his hands and feet.

Jealousy is a hitman. It kills marriages, friendships, and families. It can destroy corporations, dismantle governments, and divide nations. Jealousy will always charge you more than you want to pay and leave you with nothing to show for it. But while this green-eyed monster is a giant, our God specializes in slaying giants. And God's Word reveals how we can partner with God to slay this green-eyed monster in our own lives. We must first address how jealousy starts and how it steals, and we must then learn how to stop its power.

## CONSIDER HOW THE PROBLEM OF JEALOUSY STARTS

Let's read Proverbs 27:4 again, this time in The Message, a paraphrase of the Bible: "We're blasted by anger and swamped by rage, but who can survive jealousy?"

Jealousy is a problem we all must face and fight at some time or another, and it begins even when we're children. Remember, though, that jealousy and envy are only siblings; they're not twins. They're related, but they're different. As noted in the Merriam-Webster dictionary, "Both *jealousy* and *envy* are often used to indicate that a person is covetous of something that someone else has, but *jealousy* carries the particular sense of 'zealous vigilance' and tends to be applied more exclusively to feelings of protectiveness regarding one's own advantages or attachments."[2]

Jealousy made it possible for me to marry the girl of my dreams. Toward the end of the ninth grade, Teresa met a boy I'll call John out of respect for and for the protection of the guilty, and they started "going out." Back in the day, we called it "going steady." They were practically inseparable for the next two years. When he got his license, he drove her to school every day and then took her home after school. They also dated every weekend night and studied together most evenings. It was a storybook high school romance. He was a star on the basketball team, and she was a cheerleader. They professed their love for each other, and it was somewhat understood that they would marry after graduation and she would put him through college and medical school.

Their two-year relationship had only one problem: John was insanely jealous. He couldn't stand for Teresa to even talk to other boys, and when another boy dared to look at her, he angrily accused *her* of flirting.

One day after school, just after their senior year began, his car wouldn't start. He kept mashing the gas pedal to no avail, and Teresa rightly cautioned him not to flood the carburetor. In his exasperation he told her to shut up.

Now, in four and a half decades of marriage I have never said that to Teresa. Why? Because I've learned you don't mess around with my wife!

Teresa immediately said, "Don't talk to me that way!"

John then pulled a trick he'd used on her several times before to make her back down in an argument. "I think we should start dating other people."

Up until that time, Teresa would have shaken in fear, apologized, and professed that John was the only one for her. But not this time. She said, "I think you're right." (God is good all the time.) Then she walked back into the school and called a friend to pick her up. But unbeknownst to John, she didn't call just any friend.

Keep reading. It's about to get really good.

She called George (this time the name is changed to protect the innocent), toward whom John was more jealous than he was toward any other male on earth. George was the boy Teresa dated before John, and because of that history, John had an almost visceral dislike for George.

The plot thickens.

That was a Friday, and after Teresa told George about her fight with John, George asked Teresa to go out with him that night so he might "comfort" her and help her through this terrible turn of events. She readily agreed.

Well, that evening John had a change of heart and went to Teresa's house to patch things up with her. But when he got there, her mom (who is now my beautiful, wonderful mother-in-law!) told him Teresa was on a date. When he asked with whom, she wisely replied, "You'll have to ask her."

Beginning at 11:00 that night, Teresa's normal curfew, John began calling her only to find that she'd been granted an extra 30 minutes with George. (My in-laws always liked George, thank God!) John started calling every 10 minutes.

Finally, just after 11:30, Teresa answered, and John said, "Where have you been?"

Teresa, now realizing what she'd done, simply replied, "Out."

He then asked the dreaded question, "Who with?"

Teresa whispered, "George."

There was dead silence for about a minute, and then John uttered a promise that would be life changing and destiny altering for three people: "Teresa, I love you, but I'll die before I ever come back to you. I can't take you back with everyone knowing you went out again with George."

The dam burst as her heart broke, and rivers of tears came rushing out in a torrent. She begged. She pleaded. She asked for forgiveness. But the green-eyed monster of jealousy devoured a high school romance and opened the door for me to marry my love two years later. (If it sounds like I'm gloating, I am!)

And then there's the problem of comparison. That common spark often lights the fire of jealousy. We compare ourselves with others. We compare our house to their house, our car to their car, our paycheck to their paycheck, our spouse to their spouse.

In his book *When the Game Is Over It All Goes Back in the Box*, author John Ortberg explains that psychologists say people engage in three types of comparing. The first type is known as *downward comparison*. We compare ourselves to those we think are worse off than we are, and that can lead to arrogance. The second type is called *lateral comparison*. That's when we compare ourselves to people we perceive to be on the same level we are, and that can lead to competition. The third type is called *upward comparison*. That's when we compare ourselves to those we think are better off than we are, and that almost always leads to envy.[3] I say it can even lead to jealousy.

When jealousy sets in, we develop what I call "crab mentality." People who live near the ocean will sometimes catch crabs. You need a bucket with a lid on it so when you catch a crab the lid prevents it from crawling out. If you catch two or more crabs, you don't need a lid. Why? Because if you have two or more crabs in the bucket, every time one crab gets near the top, another crab pull him back down.

That's what jealousy does. It drives you to put other people down with your attitude, tear other people down with your words, and pull other people down with your actions. That's how the poison of jealousy enters your emotional bloodstream.

## CONSIDER HOW THE PRESENCE OF JEALOUSY STEALS

Proverbs 14:30 says, "A tranquil heart is life to the body, but jealousy is rottenness to the bones" (NASB). How about that? Jealousy rots the bones. Bones are on the inside of you. Jealousy is a corrosive that will rot you from the inside out. But if your bones rot, what do you have left? Nothing. Jealousy, Proverbs says, can steal your life.

Think about jealousy as nothing more than a common thief. Jealousy will steal the satisfaction of enjoying what you already have just because somebody else may have more of it or a better version of it. I read a story about a man who was walking along a beach and found a bottle that said *Rub me*. He rubbed it, and a genie popped out. The genie said, "Congratulations! I will grant you three wishes. You can have anything you want, but there's just one condition. I used to belong to a lawyer, so for every wish you make, every lawyer in the world will get the same thing you ask for except they will get double."

The man thought for a moment, then said, "For my first wish I want a hundred million dollars."

The genie said, "All right, but the lawyers will get two hundred million dollars. What else do you want?"

"I want to be so handsome that the most beautiful women in the world will want to have me."

"All right, but every lawyer in the world will be twice as handsome, so all the beautiful women will want them instead. What's your last wish?"

"Well, I want to donate a kidney."

You see, jealousy never gives you anything worth having. Instead, it takes away everything you have that *is* worth having.

A tree in Indonesia is called a Upas tree. This tree actually secretes poison, and it grows so full and so thick that it kills all the vegetation growing underneath it. In other words, it will give shelter and shade, but it winds up destroying everything in its path.

Jealousy is the Upas tree of life. It may make you feel good to put other people down because of your jealousy, but in the end it will poison you through and through. It will rob you of the peace you ought to have in your heart because of how God has blessed you. Instead of being happy for some other person God has blessed, you'll be resentful. You'll get depressed. You'll be angry and bitter.

The Bible tells us we ought to "rejoice with those who rejoice" and "weep with those who weep" (Romans 12:15 ESV), but when we're consumed with jealousy, we do just the opposite. We rejoice when other people weep and weep when other people rejoice.

"Comparison is the thief of joy" is a quote attributed to Theodore Roosevelt. Jealousy is the emotional kudzu of the soul. It will grow over every single part of you. It will consume you. It will control you. It will contaminate you, and eventually it will condemn you.

A professional photographer who specialized in digital imaging could really fix up photos and make people look their best. One time a woman came in with a family portrait he'd made and said, "Can you take 30 pounds off of me?"

He said, "Sure!"

He thought that was innocent enough of her until she said, "And then can you put it on my sister?"

We need to lock the doors to our heart and bar the thief of jealousy from entering, because he will take everything you have that is valuable and good.

## CONSIDER HOW THE POWER OF JEALOUSY STOPS

The green-eyed monster can be slayed in many ways. Paul knew this as someone who had many reasons to be both jealous and envious. In Philippians 4, he offers what he found to be a powerful antidote to this potentially poisonous emotion: "I have learned to be content whatever the circumstances" (verse 11).

If you believe you're where God wants you to be, if you believe you're who God wants you to be, and if you believe you have what God wants you to have, then you have no reason to ever be jealous of who someone else is, or where someone else is, or what someone else has.

Do you know what jealousy really is? It's accusing God of being unfair, playing favorites, and not giving you what you think you deserve. What you're really saying is that God has no right to bless someone differently from the way he's blessed you—that he has no right to put someone higher than you, to make someone more prosperous than you, or to promote someone other than you.

Moses is one of the greatest men in the Old Testament. He was a man of God who had God's blessing on his life. In the book of Numbers, we see that God had multiplied his ministry in the lives of 70 elders who were given the gift of prophecy. Two of those elders, named Eldad and Medad, were particularly gifted, and they began to prophesy in the camp. They were preaching powerful messages under the power of the Holy Spirit.

Joshua, who had been Moses' right-hand man since he was a young guy, came running to Moses and said, "My lord, stop them!" (Numbers 11:28). Listen to what Moses replied: "Are you jealous for my sake? I wish that all the LORD's people were prophets and that the LORD would put his Spirit on them!" (verse 29).

What was he saying to Joshua? *I'm not jealous. Why should you be? We ought to be glad that God's word is being preached in such a powerful way!*

Listen to these words from Robert Louis Stevenson quoted in Charles Swindoll's book *Living on the Ragged Edge*: "It is a good test to the rise and fall of egotism to notice how you listen the praises of other men of your own standing. Until you can listen to the praises of a rival without any desire to indulge in detraction or any attempt to belittle his work, you may be sure there is an unmortified prairie of egotistic impulse in your nature yet to be brought under the grace of God."[4]

I'm convinced that a great antidote to the poison of jealousy is contentment. Just be satisfied with what you have, with who you are, and with where you are by the grace and providence of God.

———

Every day a rich businessman drove by a fisherman who was just sitting beside his boat. He would wave to the fisherman, but the man barely acknowledged him. Finally, one day he pulled over to the side of the road, got out, walked over to the man, and said, "Do you know who I am?"

"Yes, sir. I know who you are," the fisherman said.

"Do you know how rich I am?"

"Yes, sir. You're one of the richest men in this state."

"Well, you hardly acknowledge me when I go by. Are you jealous of me?"

"Oh, sir! I'm not jealous of anybody. I think the reason I don't pay attention is because I'm thinking about how happy and satisfied I am."

The businessman said, "But why aren't you out there fishing when I drive by?"

"Because by that time I've caught all the fish I need."

"Well, why don't you catch more fish than you need?"

"What would I do with them?"

"You could sell them and earn more money. Or you could buy a bigger, better boat, go deeper, and catch more fish. You could purchase nylon nets and then catch even more fish and make more money. Soon you could buy a bunch of other boats and hire a whole bunch of other people to work for you, and then you would be rich like me and never have to worry about being jealous."

"But I told you. I'm not jealous. Besides that, if I wound up as rich as you are, then what would I do?"

"Well, you could just sit down and enjoy life," the rich man said.

The fisherman looked at him. "What do you think I do every day?"

You have a choice. You can nurture jealousy in your life and kill your contentment, or you can nurture contentment in your life and kill your jealousy. When you come to realize that the God who created you, birthed you, grew you, and guided you loved you so much that he sent his Son to die for you, then you'll know just how blessed you are. You'll have no reason to be jealous of anyone, and you will have slain the green-eyed monster right where he stood.

# BE MAD...AND GOOD

*Speak when you are angry—and you will make
the best speech you'll ever regret.*

**LAURENCE J. PETER**

Ralph Waldo Emerson, one of the greatest writers and poets in American history, said, "For every minute you remain angry, you give up sixty seconds of peace of mind." Well, I will candidly admit that I have given up more than my fair share of peace. Of all the emotions we're dealing with, this one hits home with me the hardest.

I'm not a smoldering volcano of rage, but I can get angry—and I'm not the only one. "One in five Americans reported feeling anger 'a lot' in 2018 (an increase from 17 percent in the years before) according to the Gallup 2019 Global Emotions Report."[1] And if you don't think Americans are angry, just pick your social media poison. From Facebook, to Twitter, to Instagram you had better have on some fireproof gloves or you will burn your hands!

An *Atlantic* article about American rage reported that "in 2001, just 8 percent of Americans told Pew [Researchers] they were angry at the federal government; by 2013, that number had more than tripled."[2]

He also said that "in 2012, political scientists at Emory University found that fewer than half of the voters said they were deeply angry at the other party's presidential nominee. In 2016, almost 70 percent of Americans were."[3]

You'll find a raging inferno in almost any place you go in America. There's road rage, racial rage, political rage, marital rage, vocational rage, and financial rage.

Anger is a killer in more ways than one. A *Psychology Today* article encourages us to "consider the relationship between murder and anger. There are many more killings committed spontaneously and in anger (known as voluntary manslaughter) than those committed with premeditation and after careful deliberation. In fact, first-degree murder—that is, premeditated murder committed after deliberation, is the smallest category of murder."[4]

In the same article, we learn that anger also explains why there's a tremendous gender difference in homicide: "Women are more likely to respond to strain with sadness or depression than are men who are more likely to respond with anger. Moreover, men are much more likely to express their anger in physical violence than are women. Therefore, it is no coincidence that men are responsible for nearly ninety [percent] of all murders."[5]

Now, your anger may not lead you to kill somebody, but it could wind up eventually killing you. "When a cartoon character gets angry, steam comes out the ears, red creeps over the body from head to toe, and there may even be an explosion or two. It's not as entertaining to watch in real life, but the state of anger causes physical effects in us as well."[6]

According to a study by Harvard Medical Center of Public Health, people who have angry outbursts are at an increased risk of heart attack or stroke, especially within the first two hours of getting angry: "Researchers determined that as anger levels rise, so does the risk of having a heart attack within two hours of the outburst. Moderate anger was associated with a 1.7 times greater risk of heart attack, compared to a baseline 'non-angry' state. Mid-range anger was linked to more than twice the risk. At the upper end of full-on rage, risk of heart attack within two hours jumped to 4.5 times."[7]

Another article about the health costs of anger says, "There's a direct connection between being constantly angry, hostile, and aggressive and early heart disease. In fact, over 55 hostility ratings (that is, how hostile, irritable, and angry men are toward others) predicted heart disease more accurately than any other known risk factor, including cholesterol, alcohol intake, cigarette smoking, and being overweight."[8]

When you get angry, acid pumps into your stomach, adrenaline pours into your bloodstream, your muscles tense up, and your internal organs are affected. Your physical body literally takes a beating. So it shouldn't surprise us that God's Word has a lot to say about anger. In the book of Ephesians, Paul gives a prescription for those of us who are temper-challenged to help us practice divine anger management. For many of us, by the grace of God, it can be done and it should be done and it will be done if we express sinless anger but exclude sinful anger and expel stubborn anger.

## EXPRESS SINLESS ANGER

Paul's entire message on anger is summed up in one sentence and two verses: "Be angry and do not sin; do not let the sun go down on your anger, and give no opportunity to the devil" (Ephesians 4:26-27 ESV).

The first two words may actually shock you; they shock me. Paul simply says, "Be angry." It may surprise you to know that is an imperative phrase. It's not a request; it's a command. Some things should make us angry, and sometimes we should be angry, so let it be said immediately that sin and anger are not necessarily the same thing. It's not always a sin to be angry. If it was, then Jesus would have been a sinner because he got angry on several occasions. God is a God of love, but he's also a God of anger. Sometimes being angry is one of the godliest things you can do.

You may know of an organization called MADD—Mothers Against Drunk Drivers. These mothers ought to be mad, and it's past time that the church got mad at certain things as well. What angers God should anger us, and we should never be okay with what is not okay to God. Unfortunately, though, we've lost our ability to be mad and good at the same time.

We live in a world where, every day, the shores of righteousness are flooded with the waters of wickedness, where the winds of evil and the storms of sin attack innocent hearts and homes everywhere. In fact, I would put it this way: If you're a person of character and conscience, you should be angry with wickedness and injustice. Maybe the real problem with anger is not that we sometimes get angry for the wrong reasons but that too often we don't get angry enough for the right reasons.

We ought to be mad at racial injustice. Discrimination and prejudice of any kind should have no place in our nation or our world. We should be mad at sexual immorality when God's plan for sex and marriage are decried and denied. We should be mad at the spiritual idolatry we see in a nation that has substituted gold for God, tolerance for truth, and popularity for principle. We ought to be mad at the medical iniquity of abortion, where innocent human beings who have done nothing except being conceived are taken. We should be angry about poverty and homelessness and environmental distress. We ought to be mad at the state of the church—more political at times than spiritual.

I confess I get angry because of how far short I fall of the glory of God at times. Sometimes I'm guilty of the things I preach against.

The point is righteous anger is not an option; it should be a choice we express every day.

On the other hand, Paul goes on to say, "Be angry and do not sin" (Ephesians 4:26 ESV).

That is, don't be angry in a sinful matter. There's a right way to be angry and a wrong way to be angry, but it's difficult to walk that razor-thin line. Aristotle said, "Anybody can become angry, that is easy; but to be angry with the right person, and to the right degree, and at the right time, and for the right purpose, and in the right way, that is not within everybody's power, that is not easy."[9] But he also said, "We praise a man who feels angry on the right grounds and against the right persons and also in the right matter at the right moment and for the right length of time."[10]

Some anger is wrong. First, it's wrong to be *constantly angry*. Some people are just one big hot button. They're irritable and bad tempered, and they find something to be angry about every single day. They blame it on their genetics, their upbringing, or their glands. Then it's wrong to be *quickly angry*, which is when you have a hair-trigger temper, a short fuse.

It's also wrong to be *violently angry*. You're losing total control when you begin to shake with anger, your face is white-hot, your eyes are blazing, and you become verbally and physically abusive. There's nothing wrong with anger per se, but it's wrong when we express our anger in such a way that it leads to damaging property, striking someone, injuring someone's esteem, or crushing someone's heart.

Anger can even prove to be contagious, and here's a story to illustrate that.

I'm a big New York Yankees fan. (This runs in my family. Babe Ruth married my dad's first cousin—Claire Hodgson Merritt. Look it up!) And two of my favorite Yankees were Mickey Mantle and Billy Martin. Mantle told a story about how Martin, who had just been given a new rifle, wanted to go deer hunting. Mantle had a friend he knew would allow them to hunt on his ranch near San Antonio, so they drove the several hours to get there.

When they arrived, Billy waited in the car while Mickey spoke to his friend. The friend gave Mickey permission to hunt, but he also asked him for a favor. He needed to put down a mule, but he didn't have the heart to do it himself and wanted Mickey to do it. Mickey agreed, but he also decided to have some fun with Billy.

Pretending to be angry, Mickey told Billy the man said they couldn't hunt on his property, and so he was just going to go shoot his mule. With that, he got his rifle, went to the barn, and shot the animal.

Then Mickey heard three shots ring out behind him—"Bam! Bam! Bam!" He turned around and saw Billy with his smoking rifle in his hands. He hollered, "Billy, what are you doin'?"

Billy yelled back, "I got three of his cows!"[11]

That story might strike us as funny, but the truth is your anger can influence others to be angry as well.

Either you will control your temper or your temper will control you. When your temper gets the best of you, it will always reveal the worst of you. So make sure that when you express anger, you're expressing sinless anger.

## EXCLUDE SINFUL ANGER

Some anger is sinful, and James gives us practical advice for how to exclude it from our lives.

One thing to remember is to always be slow to anger. James, the brother of Jesus, wrote "My dear brothers and sisters, take note of this: Everyone should be quick to listen, slow to speak and slow to become angry" (James 1:19). A good rule to remember is if you're getting angry, count to ten before you say anything. And if you're really angry, count to 100 and then don't say anything at all.

Wise old Ben Franklin once wrote in *Poor Richard's Almanac*, "Take it from Richard, poor and lame, what's begun in anger ends in shame."[12]

Another good rule about anger is to be quick to get rid of it. That's why Paul goes on to say, "Do not let the sun go down on your anger" (Ephesians 4:26 ESV). Anger may sometimes be a fine friend, but it's a terrible bedmate, and that's why we're specifically told it is to have a time limit. In Paul's culture the setting of the sun was considered the closing of one day and the beginning of the next day, but the point is by the end of every day you shouldn't be angry toward anyone for any reason.

I can relate to this being an accounting major in college. Paul is saying, *At the end of every day you clear all your accounts. Make sure the books are closed. You make sure the slate of your heart is wiped clean of all anger.* By the way, this will greatly help your marriage. Husbands and wives should never go to bed angry with each other. But you really shouldn't stay up and fight all night either. You should get right with each other and then go to bed.

When Teresa and I got married, we promised each other we would never ever go to bed angry. (One time we didn't sleep for four months, but we do try to never ever go to bed angry!) You can let anger sit and settle, but when you hold on to it overnight, it's like leaving milk out of the refrigerator. It will sour, and the anger will curdle into a froth of bitterness.

To put it another way, anger is like a malignant tumor, yet you will heal if you take it out. But if you don't take it out, it will metastasize and ultimately kill you both spiritually and emotionally. That's when anger truly becomes not just sinful but systemic. It will consume you, control you, and condemn you before the Lord. So you can express sinless anger, but you must exclude sinful anger.

## EXPEL STUBBORN ANGER

If you allow anger to fester, to build a nest in your heart, to take root in the soil of your soul, to become a raging river that overflows the banks of your mind, you will fall right into the hands of an invisible enemy who wants to absolutely control your life. That's why Paul concludes with this warning: "Give no opportunity to the devil" (Ephesians 4:27 ESV).

Call me old fashioned, out of date, or theologically inept, but again, I still believe in a literal being called the devil. And I'm convinced if you quit believing in him, you've fallen into his greatest trap: You won't take anything you really don't believe in seriously. Jesus believed in the devil. Paul believed in the devil. And Paul warns us to never open the door of our heart to the devil. Satan will take over your heart, kick you out, and pay no rent. You'll find yourself on the outside looking in to where God wanted you to be—in perfect harmony with him and with others.

When you allow the spark of anger to turn into a fire of bitterness, the devil will throw wood on that fire and pour kerosene on that flame. He'll make sure that fire keeps going 24/7 in your heart, in your soul, and in your mind. And that's when sinless anger can metastasize into sinful anger that becomes stubborn anger.

When God gets angry, he's always in control of his anger, and his anger is sinless. When God is in control of you, then he's in control of your anger and keeps the devil where he belongs. The moment you let the devil through the door of your heart, however, you'll no longer be in control of your anger; your anger will be in control of you.

The devil is a deceiver who will fool you into thinking that bitterness is the best way to go, that it's great to nurture your anger, to refuse to forgive and move on, to obsess over how you can get even with someone who's done you wrong. But what he doesn't tell you is that bitterness is smoking the cigarette that will give you cancer.

The devil is also a divider. The Greek word for "devil" is *diabolos*, and it comes from a verb that means "to split."[13] The devil is a splitter. The first thing Satan did was divide Adam and Eve from God. He loves to divide husbands and wives, parents and children, friends and friends, nations and nations, and church members from church members.

He's also a destroyer. Jesus called him a "murderer,"[14] and the devil loves to kill everything from joy to peace to contentment. Now, if you're a believer, you may be thinking, *Wait a minute! I thought Jesus defeated the devil at the cross? I thought his heel crushed Satan's head?* Well, he did. But remember, Satan was originally a snake, and dead snakes can still be deadly. Here's an incident report that proves the point:

> A chef who was mixing up a spitting cobra soup dish was killed [when] the decapitated head from the snake bit him—20 minutes after it was removed from the snake's body... The chef had already made and served [the soup], when he went to throw the head into the garbage. That's when it bit him, injecting him with fast acting venom...The chef died before he was able to get anti-venom in a hospital.[15]

*The New England Journal of Medicine* published a study concerning people bitten by dead snakes. They discovered that 15 percent of people admitted to hospitals for a snake bite were bitten by a dead snake. Snakes have a reflex action that continues even after being killed, and for this reason a decapitated rattlesnake can still bite up to an hour after its death.[16]

Even if you think he's completely dead, the devil still has a bite. You can ignore him or think he doesn't exist, but he's still deadly. That's why you need to make sure you don't give place to the devil but put the devil in his place.

———

How can you be mad and good? Here are three practical ways to do it:

1. *Confront* your anger. When you feel anger rising up in you, call it what it is. Meet it head-on. Realize exactly what's happening the moment your temper rears its ugly head. Make sure you have a righteous reason to be angry, and if deep down you know you don't, don't excuse your anger.

2. *Confess* your anger. If you feel yourself getting angry at the wrong time, in the wrong place, at the wrong person, or for the wrong reason, don't try to hide it, camouflage it, or justify it. Confess it to the Lord immediately. Look at your anger through his eyes and see it for what it is.

3. *Confine* your anger. Limit the duration of your anger. Don't let the sun go down on it. Limit the direction of your anger. Be angry at the problem, not the person. Finally, limit the dimension of your anger. Never fly into a rage. Social commentator Will Rogers said people who do "always make a bad landing."

You may think you can't control your anger, but you can allow God to control you. The God who through his Son, Jesus Christ, conquered death can conquer your anger as well. If you will simply be like him, you can be mad...and good.

# PUSH AWAY THE PULL OF PUNISHMENT

*Bitterness is how we punish ourselves for other people's sins.*

**MATSHONA DHLIWAYO**

On Father's Day morning 1999, Ron Shanabarger jumped into the shower, and instead of doing it himself as he normally would, he asked his wife, Amy, to get up their seven-month-old son, Tyler. When Amy walked into their son's bedroom, she found little Tyler lying face down in his crib, stiff and cold. Amy screamed and called 911, but it was too late. The autopsy listed the cause of death as SIDS—Sudden Infant Death Syndrome. The couple buried Tyler two days later.

After the funeral, Amy sat on her living room couch sobbing. She was racked with guilt, wondering if she could have saved their son.

Then Ron told her this unbelievable story. While that precious little baby boy was playing with his feet in the crib, Ron had wrapped his head in plastic wrap. Then after he ate dinner and brushed his teeth, he returned just in time to see his son take his last breath. He removed the wrap, turned the baby onto his stomach, turned off the light, and went to bed.

In shock, Amy asked why he'd done such a thing.

His answer? "Now we're even."

Ron said he'd never forgiven her for not returning early from an ocean cruise with her parents when his father died three years earlier. He'd wanted her to be there to comfort him. Then he told her he decided to marry her, have a child with her, and then kill it.[1]

So what left behind the wreckage and carnage of a dead seven-month-old boy, a broken marriage, a shattered wife and mother, and a 49-year prison sentence for a husband and father? One word: bitterness.

Anger and bitterness are closely related. They're next of kin, but they're not twins. Let me give you the major differences between the two.

- Anger leaves quickly; bitterness lingers indefinitely.

- Most of the time you can count to ten and get past your anger, but you can count to a million and never get past your bitterness.

- Anger is sometimes good; bitterness never is.

- Anger is a normal emotion and can be good if it's used the right way, at the right time, in the right place, with the right person. It can produce good results. Bitterness provides no value.

- We can control anger; bitterness controls us.

- Anger may control you temporarily; bitterness will consume you totally.

- Anger is about the present; bitterness is about the past.

- Anger takes up only today; bitterness takes up your past, present, and future.

- Anger is aboveground; bitterness is underground.

Now, what is bitterness? Here's my definition: *Bitterness is harbored hurt hidden in the heart.* Of all the emotions I cover in this book, I believe this one may be the most dangerous. I fear bitterness in my life more than anything else. Do you know why? Because bitterness is an acid that destroys its own container.

I'm certain I'm speaking to people right now who are in bondage to the master of bitterness. Maybe you're bitter toward God because of a tragedy in your life he didn't prevent. Perhaps you're bitter toward a spouse who left you for someone else and made you a single parent raising children on your own. Maybe you're bitter toward a company that fired you with no severance even though you served them faithfully for many years. Maybe you're bitter toward someone who physically or sexually abused you but never admitted it and will never be brought to justice. Maybe you're bitter toward a father who never gave you any approval or a mother who never affirmed her love for you. Maybe you're bitter toward a church because of a bad experience.

In the New Testament book of Hebrews, we find a strong warning about the danger of bitterness, and in the twelfth chapter we encounter practical wisdom for how to deal with bitterness. You may be bitter now, but if you apply three pieces of wise advice—uncover the root of bitterness, understand the root of bitterness, and undertake the removal of bitterness—you can push away the pull of bitterness.

## UNCOVER THE ROOT OF BITTERNESS

Hebrews 12:15 says, "See to it that no one falls short of the grace of God and that no bitter root grows up to cause trouble and defile many."

The metaphor for bitterness here is a root, and you don't have to be a botanist to know a tree root exists beneath the surface. The trunk branches, leaves, and fruit are all visible to you, but you can't see the roots unless you dig. But roots are just as real as the tree they support.

A root, even though it's not far from the surface, stretches deep into the soil. Bitterness is just like that; it's never far from the surface of your lips or your life, but it reaches deep into the soil of your heart.

Just like any root has a seed and lives in soil, so does bitterness. Where does the root of bitterness come from? Remember, *bitterness is harbored hurt hidden in the heart.* The seed of bitterness is your hurt, and the soil of bitterness is your heart.

When people are bitter, they allow their hurt to plant itself in the heart and grow roots. But even worse, they fertilize it, cultivate it, feed it, water it, and grow entangled with it. When that happens, the fruit becomes as bitter as the root. The fruit is negativity, a critical spirit, judgmentalism, fault-finding, and revenge. The invisible root is made visible by the fruit. And that's what's so interesting about bitterness: Although it's a root we can't see, it always bears fruit we can see.

Bitterness will find its root in your heart, but it will bear its fruit in your life. That's why so many people deal with a hair-trigger temper, impatience, depression, a negative spirit, and even physical ailments. They go to doctors and therapists, but they never solve the problem because they're dealing with only the symptoms. To solve the problem, you have to get to the root of the problem. You've got to go to the heart of your bitterness because bitterness is always the problem of the heart.

Years ago, in a tiny village in a remote part of Africa, children and adults were overcome with nausea. Several weeks went by, and the sickness spread and people started dying. When the disease got back to the main city in that area, they sent in experts to try to determine what was causing the problem. They soon discovered that the water there was contaminated. The village got its water supply from a mountain stream fed from a spring, so the experts decided to go upstream to try to find the source of the pollution.

They finally came to the mouth of the stream, but on the surface, they didn't find anything wrong. So they hired some divers to go beneath the surface to get to the opening of the spring to see what was going on. What the divers discovered shocked everyone. A large mother pig and her baby piglets were wedged right at the opening of the spring. Evidently, they had fallen in and drowned and somehow been stuck there. All of that clear, pure mountain spring water was being contaminated as it flowed past the decomposing remains of those dead pigs.

When they extricated the dead pigs, the water began to flow clean and pure once again, and the disease disappeared. The problem was not on the surface of the water or even in the water; it was at the spring where the water came out. That was the root of the problem.

Very few bitter people will ever admit they're bitter. I can't tell you the number of times I've dealt with bitter people who would swear they weren't bitter on a stack of Bibles. You can't see the root of it, but you can sure see the fruit of it. Let me encourage you to uncover the root of your bitterness.

## UNDERSTAND THE RESULT OF BITTERNESS

Hebrews 12:15 tells us if that bitter root is allowed to grow up, it will "cause trouble and defile many." A bitter root always bears bitter fruit, and everywhere you go, your bitterness will go with you and cause you trouble. It will affect every part of you. It will affect your relationship with God, with others, and even with yourself. It will affect you on the inside and the outside—mentally, emotionally, physically, and spiritually.

### Bitterness will affect you mentally.

As the root of bitterness grows, it takes up more and more of the soil of your heart. Just like jealousy is emotional kudzu, bitterness is mental kudzu. It will take over your mind. When you're bitter toward someone, you carry a mental picture of that person around with you everywhere you go. You think about them constantly. You dream about how you can hurt them or how they could be hurt. You spend waking moments thinking about how you can get even with them.

When you've got an internal conflict because of an external conflict you've had with someone else, it will affect you psychologically until you resolve it. There's even a term for this: the Zeigarnik Effect. This refers to the brain's process of keeping unresolved issues under "active status." Once a task is successfully completed, the brain will file it into a special memory, and it is no longer given priority attention.

When you have a situation that hasn't been resolved, your brain will keep that on active file until a solution is found. Here's an example: Did you ever see a person you knew but you just couldn't remember their name, and then an hour or two later the name came back to you? That's because your brain wouldn't let it go.

Bitterness has the same effect. Your brain or your mind will not let it go until that bitterness is resolved.

### Bitterness will affect you emotionally.

Doctors now know that bitterness acts like a depressant. You know, in all of my years, I've never met a bitter person who was happy. Bitter people are critical, negative, and fault-finding, and they have a victim mentality.

A surefire mark of a bitter person is that they play what I call "the blame and shame game." It doesn't matter what's happened to them; it's always somebody else's fault. They're never responsible for anything. They're always the innocent party. They think they never have anything to apologize for. They think everyone has done them harm, but they don't see the harm they've done to others much less to themselves.

All this is why bitterness is so dangerous. It will cause you to burn down your house to kill a rat. It will turn you into an emotional suicide bomber. You want to hurt others, but you wind up killing yourself. My favorite definition of bitterness is *a bitter person is someone who drinks poison and hopes the other person dies.*

Nelson Mandela stated it perfectly: "Bitterness only hurts one's self. If you hate, you will give them your heart and mind. Don't give those two things away."[2]

### Bitterness will affect you physically.

Your body was not created to nourish bitterness. Your back was never built to carry grudges. Doctors now know over 50 diseases, ranging from ulcers to high blood pressure, can be caused by bitterness.

In his book *Grace Is Greater*, Kyle Idleman shared that a *New York Times* article said, "Researchers have gathered a wealth of data largely suggesting that chronic anger is so damaging to the body that it ranks with—or even exceeds—cigarette smoking, obesity, and a high-fat diet as a powerful risk factor for early death."[3] He also said that "in a study at the University of Michigan, a group of women were tested to determine which were harboring longterm bitterness. Then all the women were tracked for eighteen years, and the outcome was startling: women, with suppressed anger and bitterness were three times more likely to have died during the study than those who did not have bitter hostility."[4]

Two famous clinical doctors, Frank Minirth and Paul Meier, researched 10,000 patients who were burned out. They had either just quit their job or had all but decided to give up on life itself. They diagnosed the top three reasons for their burnout, and the results were amazing. The number one reason people burned out was not stress, nor was it overwork. The number one cause of physical and emotional burnout was bitterness. Being unwilling to forgive and let go of a grudge was the dominant cause of burnout.[5]

*Bitterness will affect you spiritually.*

Hebrews 12:14-15 says, "Make every effort to live in peace with everyone and to be holy; without holiness no one will see the Lord. See to it that no one falls short of the grace of God." Inwardly, with bitterness there will be nothing but turmoil, and there will be tension with you and other people. But upwardly, there will be trouble between you and God. You won't find peace, joy, or happiness whether you look in the mirror, outside the window, or up to the sky. Bitterness is a spiritual heartburn you will carry with you everywhere you go.

Bitterness can not only ruin your life in the present but can follow you to the grave. Following the death of a 94-year-old who had never married, this notice appeared in the church bulletin: "There will be no male pallbearers. They wouldn't take me out when I was alive; I don't want them to take me out when I'm dead."[6]

That story might make us laugh, but bitterness is no laughing matter. And you won't be the only one affected by your bitterness. Remember, the root of bitterness "grows up to cause trouble and defile many" (Hebrews 12:15). Bitterness never hurts just one person. I've seen marriages, friendships, and other relationships destroyed by bitterness. If you're going to defeat this monster that destroys everything in its path, you not only must uncover the root of it but understand the result of it.

## UNDERTAKE THE
## REMOVAL OF BITTERNESS

I heard someone describe bitterness as a prison. They pointed out that when you put somebody in the jail cell of your bitterness, you're stuck guarding the door.

You need to understand this: The only way to get free of bitterness is to free the person you're bitter toward. Then you will be free yourself. If you refuse to open the jail door of your bitterness and let your prisoner out, you're the one who suffers. You're the one paying for your bitterness. You're the one losing sleep. You're the one developing ulcers. You're the one who can't enjoy life because you live under the searing heat of bitterness every day. You're the one who's miserable. You're thinking about the person you're bitter toward, and they aren't giving a thought to you.

Once again, the author of Hebrews says, "See to it that…no bitter root grows up" (Hebrews 12:15). So as the great Mayberry philosopher Barney Fife frequently said, "You've got to nip it in the bud."[7] To do that you've got to remember bitterness is a root that's underground, and that means you've got to find it, dig it up, and throw it away. That's why the only cure for the pull of bitterness is what I call a "spiritual root canal."

If you've ever had a root canal (which I have), then you know it's not pleasant. But it is necessary to save a tooth that's either decayed or infected. The dentist removes the nerve and pulp from inside of the tooth, then cleans it out completely, removing the decay and infection. Then the dentist seals that tooth so the infection can never return. The only alternative is to lose the tooth.

So how is that done spiritually? First, forgive the guilty party, and then, as much as possible, forget what happened.

### Forgive the one who hurt you.

The first thing you must do is forgive. Doctors and psychiatrists now know the only cure for the cancer of bitterness is the chemotherapy of forgiveness. Someone once defined forgiveness as *giving up my right to hurt you for hurting me*. If you don't, as the author of Hebrews puts it, you will "fall short of the grace of God" (Hebrews 12:15).

Now, what did he mean by that? He simply meant that until you go back to the cross of Christ and remember how the grace of God has forgiven you, you will not forgive others. You will never forgive someone for what they've done to you until you experience how God has forgiven you for what you've done to him. Someone who has experienced the grace of God and lives in the grace of God has the power to forgive others by the grace of God.

We can all relate to this story told in a sermon on the tenth anniversary of 9/11. An American soldier serving his country in Afghanistan received a Dear John letter from the girl he was going to marry, saying she'd found someone else. To add insult to injury, she also said, *Please return my favorite picture of myself, because I would like to use that photograph for my engagement picture in the county newspaper.*

He was devastated, but he was also hot, and he began to think about how he could get even with her.

His buddies came to his defense. When what happened came out to his platoon, they went throughout the barracks and collected photos of all the other soldiers' girlfriends and filled an entire shoebox with them. The soldier mailed the photos to his ex-girlfriend with this note: *Please find your enclosed picture and return the rest. For the life of me, I can't remember which one you were.*[8]

The truth of the matter is you never get even in the way you hope. When you try to, you just pull yourself down to the level of the person who hurt you to begin with. But you can forgive by the grace of God. Indeed, once you've experienced the forgiveness of God, you can forgive others.

## To the degree it's possible and even wise, forget the offense.

God forgets our transgressions—"I am he who blots out your transgressions for my own sake, and I will not remember your sins" (Isaiah 43:25 ESV)—and forgetting transgressions against us should be our goal as well. As much as possible, they should be forgotten and buried for everyone's sake, including ours.

But hear this caution: Some offenses are so egregious that they're either not easily forgotten or can never be completely forgotten. In some cases, for the physical and emotional protection of the person hurt and who could be hurt again, they *shouldn't* be forgotten even though reconciliation on some level is a possibility. Examples are the abuse of a child and rape by a family member. If you've suffered such an offense, a Christian therapist can assist you with not only the process of forgiveness but dealing with its impact on your life.

But bitterness in your heart *does* need to be released. Ephesians 4:31 says, "Get rid of all bitterness, rage and anger, brawling and slander, along with every form of malice." That phrase *get rid of* means to "dispose of" or "to bury."[9] At the very least, you've got to get that "get even" feeling out of your heart. You've got to bury that root of bitterness in an unmarked grave and forget where you buried it.

———

In her book *Unbroken*, Laura Hillebrand tells a story that illustrates how forgiven people can forgive others.

Louis Zamperini was a world-famous Olympian who was captured as a prisoner of war in Japan. When the head of the prison camp, Watanabe, nicknamed the Bird Man, found out who he was, he decided to pour all of his wrath, hatred, and torture on Zamperini. He made his life a living hell 24/7. Zamperini grew to hate this man more than he cared for his own life or his own freedom. Though he survived his captivity physically, he didn't survive emotionally.

When he came home he began to drink. He was so consumed with hatred for the Bird Man that every night he dreamed about killing this man. Then Zamperini went to a Billy Graham crusade, heard the gospel, and truly experienced the forgiveness and grace of God. Amazingly, decades later, Louis was asked to return to Japan to carry the Olympic torch for the United States. He wondered if this brutal prison camp warden Watanabe was alive and found out he was. As he thought and prayed through his visit, he sat down at his computer and wrote this letter:

> To Mutsuhiro Watanabe,
>
> As a result of my prisoner of war experience under your unwarranted and unreasonable punishment, my post-war life became a nightmare. It was not so much due to the pain and suffering as it was the tension of stress and humiliation that caused me to hate you with a vengeance.
>
> Under your discipline, my rights, not only as a prisoner of war but also as a human being, were stripped from me. It was a struggle to maintain enough dignity and hope to live until the war's end.
>
> The post-war nightmares caused my life to crumble, but thanks to a confrontation with God through the evangelist Billy Graham, I committed my life to Christ. Love has replaced the hate I had for you. Christ said, "Forgive your enemies and pray for them."
>
> As you probably know, I returned to Japan in 1952 and was graciously allowed to address all the Japanese war criminals at Sugamo Prison...I asked then about you, and was told that you probably had committed Hara Kiri, which I was sad to hear. At that moment, like the others, I also forgave you and now would hope that you would also become a Christian.
>
> Louis Zamperini

Louis carried the letter to Japan and asked to meet with Watanabe. But when CBS contacted him and asked if Zamperini could come and see him, he practically spit out "No!" with gritted teeth and anger in his face. Someone took the letter from Louis and got it to Watanabe, but he never replied to it.[10]

These two men are now dead, but as far as we know, only one of them died free of bitterness.

The bottom line is you can be full of bitterness and empty of Jesus or full of Jesus and empty of bitterness, but you can't be both. Being bitter is no way to live, and being bitter is no way to die, but by the grace of God you can push away the punishment of bitterness—a punishment that affects not only others but you as well.

# SEEK A CLEAN SLATE

*No guilt is forgotten so long as the conscience still knows of it.*
STEFAN ZWEIG

It's one thing to have a throbbing headache, but it's an entirely different thing to have a permanently throbbing headache. Li Fuyan could testify to the misery it caused him. No doubt this Chinese man had seen every doctor and every specialist. He'd tried every treatment you could imagine to rid him of his headache, but nothing worked. Finally, an X-ray revealed the problem everyone had missed. Four years earlier he'd weathered an attack by a robber, and the robber's knife blade had broken off inside his skull. For four years a rusty four-inch piece of metal had been lodged there without his knowing it.[1]

When there's a foreign object inside your body that doesn't belong there, your body is designed to alert you by generating pain until it's removed. And what's true of the body is even more true of the soul. We all deal with a particular emotion at times, and in fact, some of us live with it every day.

It can wake us up in the middle of night and even keep us from going to sleep. Left untreated, it can drive us mad. It's like a ghost that haunts every hallway of our life. It's the face we see every time we look in the mirror. It's a dark cloud that hovers over our head on the sunniest of days. And soon we'll find we can't run from it much less hide from it.

Once it's removed, however, we can experience a release—a freedom—that's purely exhilarating. I'm talking about guilt. And, yes, it's operable. It's curable.

In this chapter we'll be touching some tender nerves. Do you feel regret for the way you treated your sibling the last time you spoke? Do you have remorse because of the way your marriage ended? Are you tortured over the person you could have helped, that you should have helped, but didn't? Or maybe you're plagued by a secret you've been keeping all of your life.

My first memory of feeling guilt is from the first grade. My mother was a hairdresser, and when she went to work on Saturdays, a sweet lady named Mrs. Gunter watched me at her house. She became like a second mother to me. Her son, Scotty, was away at college, and he had a soldier's hat in his bedroom. I loved that hat, and one day as I was getting ready to go home, I grabbed it, hid it under my shirt, and smuggled it home.

The only problem was I couldn't actually wear the hat. If my mom or dad asked me where I got it, I'd have to rat myself out. So I hid it under my bed.

For the next week, I got the worst nights' sleep of my life. That hat didn't make me happy; it made me miserable. I soon came to realize I didn't have the hat; the hat had me. I don't even know if I could have defined the word *guilt* at age six, but that's when I learned how it felt. I couldn't wait until the next Saturday.

When Mom dropped me off at Mrs. Gunter's house, I walked into her kitchen with that hat, set it on the kitchen table, and with tears in my eyes said, "Mrs. Gunter, I stole Scotty's hat, and I'm so sorry."

She came over to me and said, "I knew you took the hat, and I knew you would bring it back. I forgive you." Then I had the best time of my life playing, and I had the best night's sleep I'd had in a week.

You may be living with guilt today, but you don't have to live with guilt tomorrow. Let me say up front that there is no human cure for the problem of guilt. That's because the cause of all legitimate guilt is sin, and only God can deal with sin. Sin is the wound. Guilt is the infection. God alone has the cure.

A king named David practically had a PhD in guilt. This demon tortured him for an entire year of his life, and David wrote a song about it called Psalm 51. The occasion for this song is found in the introduction to it: "A psalm of David. When the prophet Nathan came to him after David had committed adultery with Bathsheba."

God used Nathan as the judge and jury in David's case, and David heard the one word a defendant never wants to hear in a courtroom: "Guilty!" But he'd finally come face-to-face with not only his adulterous affair with another man's wife but the innocent husband's murder, which he'd engineered.

David's song answers this question: When you're confronted, caught, and convicted of sin in your life and you no longer want to run from God but to God, what do you do? This psalm tells us how we can say goodbye to guilt and gain a clean slate: confess your guilt, process your grief, and access God's grace.

## CONFESS YOUR GUILT

The first step to cleaning the slate is to quit running from your guilt. In fact, you've got to run *to* it. You've got to uncover what you've covered and fess up to your mess up. And in this psalm, David starts the process toward the necessary surgery to remove this guilt from his heart.

I recently had surgery. But first was the pre-op, when I was asked certain questions to ensure they were operating on the right person for the right reason.

"Why are you here?" they asked me.

"Shoulder surgery."

"Which shoulder?"

"Right one."

"Why are you having this surgery?"

"Except for two torn rotator cuffs, a bicep muscle torn from the tendon, and gigantic bone spurs, I have no idea!"

In the first two verses of this psalm, we see David's pre-op: "Have mercy on me, O God, according to your unfailing love; according to your great compassion blot out my transgressions. Wash away all my iniquity and cleanse me from my sin" (Psalm 51:1-2).

Notice that David confronts his problem right up front. You've got to take sin seriously. Sin is not a misdemeanor; it's a felony. It's not a cold; it's a cancer. David uses three different words to describe what caused his guilt to begin with.

The word *transgression* means to "cross a forbidden boundary" or "to rebel against the law."[2] David had crossed a line he shouldn't have crossed and broken a law he should have kept.

The word *iniquity* means "perversity."[3] It's just perverse to think that you can sin against an all-knowing, ever-present God and get away with it.

The word *sin* means to "miss the mark."[4] The bull's-eye of your life should be the will of God, because that's always what's best for you, and because sin always falls short of God's best. David doesn't call sin a "mistake," a "misfortune," or a "misjudgment." He calls it what God calls it: sin. And the word *confess* means to agree with God on exactly what sin is. So it's not an affair; it's adultery. It's not fudging the figures; it's lying. It's not borrowing indefinitely; it's stealing.

Now that David has confronted the cause of his guilt, he's ready for surgery to deal with the problem of his guilt: "I know my transgressions, and my sin is always before me. Against you, you only, have I sinned and done what is evil in your sight; so you are right in your verdict and justified when you judge" (Psalm 51:3-4).

The only knife sharp enough to cut through the skin of sin and get rid of the tumor of guilt is the knife of confession. One thing God will never accept for any sin is an excuse. You cannot alibi your way out of sin; it just makes the tumor grow and the cancer metastasize. When you try to cover the sin that caused your guilt, God will uncover it. But when you finally uncover the sin that caused your guilt, God will cover it.

You may have heard of Lecrae Moore, a Grammy Award–winning hip-hop artist who has a tremendous influence for Christ and has publicly admitted the role he played in persuading his then girlfriend to abort their child in 2002. He says he had converted to Christianity at the time, but he was still in the lifestyle of drugs and sex and promiscuity. When he dropped his girlfriend off at the abortion clinic, he sensed it was wrong, but he chose his life over his child's.

In a 2015 interview, Lecrae said that years before he wrote a song about this experience, titled "Good, Bad, Ugly," he was preparing to marry the woman who is now his wife when he found a photo of his ex-girlfriend. He said, "I literally broke down over the guilt and the remorse and the shame of it all. That was the beginning of the healing process for me."[5]

The moment we do something wrong and feel guilty about it, our first instinct is to run and hide and get away from the shame of it. How often do you see somebody who's been arrested and is most likely guilty attempting to hide their face or turn away from the camera because they don't want anybody to see who they are and know what they've done? The problem with guilt is that when you run away from it, you not only carry it with you but the burden grows heavier and the pain gets greater.

Now, to be clear, there are two kinds of guilt—undeserved guilt and legitimate, deserved guilt. Undeserved guilt is when you feel guilty even though you're not guilty. Undeserved guilt is never from God. An example is what's called "survivor's guilt," which occurs when a person feels like they've done wrong just by surviving a traumatic event. Some sufferers are people who survived the Holocaust, or survived combat, or survived a plane crash. They feel guilty because they lived when other people died. The only thing God will convict you of is sin that you purposely committed and haven't confessed. Otherwise, the guilt you feel is false guilt.

On the other hand, understand that one of God's gifts to us is the ability to feel guilty. Simply put, deserved guilt is good guilt. Good guilt has been called the nerve ending of the heart.[6] Guilt is God's way of telling us that we're driving a car out of line, singing a song out of tune, and playing an instrument off key. It's his way of getting us back on track.

## PROFESS YOUR GRIEF

David gets to the heart of the matter when he tells God, "Against you, you only, have I sinned and done what is evil in your sight; so you are right in your verdict and justified when you judge" (Psalm 51:4).

There's no such thing as a sin that doesn't hurt anybody. Sin always hurts God. Take David's sin with Bathsheba. Even if the sex had been consensual, even if Bathsheba had been a single woman, the moment David had relations with her he not only broke God's law but broke his heart.

In this next verse David tells God the most basic reason he sinned: "Surely I was sinful at birth, sinful from the time my mother conceived me" (verse 5).

We all sin because we're all born sinners. We do what we do because we're what we are. David doesn't want to deal with just the symptoms of the problem; he wants to deal with the cause of it.

A Bible teacher trying to teach his class of first graders about the nature of sin said, "Boys and girls, do you understand we are all born in sin?" One little girl looked confused, so he said, "Sarah, what's wrong?"

"I wasn't born in sin," she told him. "I was born in November."

The truth is we're all born in sin. David committed adultery because in his heart he was an adulterer. He lied because in his heart he was a liar. He murdered because in his heart he was a murderer.

That's why every person is born with a spiritual congenital heart defect and we all need a spiritual heart transplant. We need a new heart, and you can't buy those on Amazon. They don't stock them at IKEA. It's not a prescription your pharmacist can fill. Only one doctor can heal your problem of guilt, and that's the Great Physician—God.

For a year, David had been miserable living in the filth of his sin and the misery of his guilt. When he was in public, he put on the face of a king, winning what amounted to an Academy Award for Best Actor every day of his life. But it was just an act. He put on the face of gladness with a heart of sadness.

But the good news is this did prove he was one of God's children. It proved he truly did have a love for God. I believe the saddest, most miserable people I've ever met are not atheists or playboys—people who frankly enjoy a life of sin, doing their own thing, being their own boss. The most miserable people I've ever met are people who love God, who know God, but live in unconfessed, unforgiven, unforsaken sin and are eaten up with the cancer of guilt.

I feel sorry for anyone who's committed a crime like murder. It's a tragedy to see people incarcerated for an egregious act, with all but a few most likely wasting their life. But the criminals I feel most sorry for are the ones who show no remorse, no regret.

A defendant was on trial for murder with strong evidence that he was guilty. But there was no corpse, and in his closing argument his defending attorney pointed out that the man felt no remorse because he was innocent. Still, fearing his client would most likely be convicted, the attorney resorted to a trick he had up his sleeve.

Looking at his watch, he said, "Ladies and gentlemen of the jury, I have a surprise for you all. Within one minute, the murder victim will walk into the courtroom, and this case will be over!"

He looked toward the courtroom door, and the stunned jurors joined him. After the minute passed, the lawyer triumphantly said, "I actually made that up. But you all looked with anticipation, and that proves you have a reasonable doubt as to whether a murder has taken place. That means you must return a verdict of 'not guilty'!" He smugly sat down and received a slap on the back from his giddy client.

The jury retired to deliberate, and only 10 minutes later they returned with a verdict of guilty. Both lawyer and defendant were stunned as the man was led away in handcuffs. Afterward, the attorney said to the jury foreman, "How did you reach a guilty verdict and so soon? I saw you all stare at the door, so you must have had doubt!"

The foreman replied, "Oh, we did look, but your client didn't!"

Understand this: You can be remorseful but not repentant, but you can't be repentant if you're not remorseful. When you break God's heart, he won't rest until he breaks your heart so you'll admit your grief. Indeed, God will do what's necessary for you to see your guilt clearly and cleanly.

A lady who was a hypochondriac visited her doctor with a new complaint every week. One week the doctor said, "Mrs. Smith, what's wrong with you today?"

"It's my hearing. It's so bad I can't hear myself cough."

The doctor wrote out a prescription and gave it to her.

She said, "Will this improve my hearing?"

"No, but it will help you cough louder."

When you're guilty, God will make you cough louder until you hear his voice and admit your grief. Then you'll be ready to take the next step.

## ACCESS GOD'S GRACE

Remember where guilt comes from. The first person who ever felt guilty about anything was Adam. He'd broken God's law, and he'd broken God's heart, but he was created to bless God's heart. He was also created without the ability to handle guilt, and he didn't know how to deal with it. So he did what we all do—he ran and he hid.

The best doctors, surgeons, psychiatrists, counselors, psychologists, advisors, and medicines in the entire world can't cure guilt. Forgiveness is the only cure, and there's only one source of total, true forgiveness—God. Even though guilt is an inside job, you've got to have outside help to get over it. All sin is against God, and you're never truly forgiven until God forgives you first.[7]

To use a medical analogy, sin is a spiritual toxin that poisons our heart and our mind. It infuses the bloodstream of our soul with guilt, and on our own we're helpless to get rid of it. To use a modern term, we require a *divine detox*.

David knows the only remedy for the guilt and grief sin brings is the grace of God. So as we noted earlier, he first says to God, "Have mercy on me, O God, according to your unfailing love; according to your great compassion blot out my transgressions" (Psalm 51:1).

Sin leaves a record, and David wants the slate wiped clean. That word *blot* refers to the removing of writing from a book or an indictment from a file. David needed God to delete all of his sin from the memory of his hard drive. The only thing David could do was what he needed to do—go to the only One who could wipe the slate clean: God.

Then in verse 2, David said, "Wash away all my iniquity." Sin doesn't just make you guilty; it makes you dirty. In fact, that's what sin feels like to a healthy conscience—filthy and dirty. Like the prodigal son, you wind up in the pigpen of life and want to take a spiritual shower. You want to get under the faucet of God's forgiveness and under the pipeline of his pardon. You want to come clean so you will be clean. So David logically asks God to "cleanse" him from his sin.

The word *cleanse* means to "purge."[8] It means "de-sin me." David is asking for a divine detox because he knows that's the only thing that will release him from his guilt. You see, you don't just need a pardon for your sin; you need purity from your sin. You don't just need to be cleared of your sin; you need to be cleansed from your sin.

In verse 10, David goes on to says, "Create in me a pure heart, O God, and renew a steadfast spirit within me." He realizes guilt is not just a fungus on the surface of the skin you can scrape off or an irritation you can cure with a home remedy. It takes a heart remedy. It takes radical surgery. It takes a spiritual heart transplant. In fact, it really takes a miracle. The word for "create" is the same word used in Genesis to describe the creation of the world.[9] Only one surgeon has the skilled hands and the compassionate heart that can remove the guilt from your soul: Dr. God.

We need to say goodbye to guilt and have the slate wiped clean, because here's what David learned the hard way:

- Guilt beats you up and leaves you for dead; forgiveness picks you up and restores you to health.

- Sin sinks you into guilt; forgiveness raises you with grace.

- Sin banishes God outside; forgiveness invites God inside.

- Sin will cost you everything and give you a guilty conscience; forgiveness cost God everything but gives you a clean heart.

Remember, you won't be able to accept God's grace until you admit your guilt and acknowledge your grief. Perhaps the best-known hymn in the world is "Amazing Grace." You will never realize how amazing grace is until you realize how terrible your guilt is. As long as you think *I'm not that bad*, grace will never seem all that good.

Now, you may be thinking, *I feel guilty because I am guilty. I'm addicted to drugs* [or maybe porn]. *I've cheated on my spouse* [or maybe your taxes]. *I've blown it with my kids* [or maybe with your parents]. This is where the cross of Christ and the grace of God come in. Jesus came to this earth, lived a perfect life, died on a cross, and came back from the grave to pay for your sins and give you the forgiveness you desperately need. He didn't come to reject you; he came to release you, renew you, revive you, and restore you. The only sin God can't forgive is the sin of refusing to ask for his forgiveness because one is either unwilling to admit they are a sinner in need of a savior or believe their goodness so outweighs their badness (or eliminates it altogether) they see no need for God's forgiveness.

No matter how deep the stain of your guilt is, one drop of God's amazing grace can give you a clean slate for the asking and the taking. If you need that clean slate, seek it now.

PART TWO

# LIFE GIVERS

# I BELIEVE

*All I have seen teaches me to trust the*
*Creator for all I have not seen.*

**RALPH WALDO EMERSON**

So far we've covered the gamut of most of the major negative emotions that debilitate our moods, discourage our optimism, and deceive us into thinking we're trapped in defeat and despair forever. Well, allow me to say this before we go on: *That's just a feeling! It's not a fact.*

Perhaps as you read through the chapters in Part One, "Life Takers," you found yourself agreeing with most if not all I said, but you still don't see the light at the end of the tunnel. If I were to ask you what you want from God, you most likely would answer, "To deliver me from [fill in the blank]," be it stress, worry, anxiety, depression, fear, loneliness, jealousy, anger, bitterness, guilt, or any other challenging emotion.

Have you ever considered that perhaps God wants you to ask yourself this question before he will grant your request? *What does God want from me?* Well, according to a passage in the book of Hebrews, we don't have to wonder. The answer is *faith*, the first of our "life givers" in Part Two of this book.

From the beginning of time, faith is what God has always wanted from us, and the road to a relationship with him is paved with faith. The first followers of Jesus weren't called Christians at first; they were called believers. And even in the toughest and darkest of times, God wants to hear us say, *I believe.*

I believe one of the reasons negative feelings attack us, bedevil us, and perhaps at times consume and control us is that we don't truly have faith that God can solve the problem, answer the question, or heal the hurt causing those negative emotions to begin with. Put simply, I'm convinced that the antidote to negative feelings begins with a positive faith in an all-knowing, all-seeing, all-hearing, ever-present God who doesn't want us to waste our lives wallowing in negative feelings but to walk in the positive joy and excitement of trusting him in all things and for all things.

To that end, using this passage in Hebrews, I'm asking you to affirm or reaffirm your faith in three things and then act as if you do regardless of your feelings.

## I BELIEVE IN A GOD
## WHO IS REASONABLE

In Hebrews, faith is described this way: "Faith is confidence in what we hope for and assurance about what we do not see" (11:1).

Notice two key words that go along with the word *faith*. One is *confidence*, and the other is *assurance*. *Confidence* comes from a Greek word that means "to stand under" or "something to stand on."[1] In other words, it's a foundation. The point is faith is solid. It has substance, and it's based on substance.

Many will tell you there is no substance to faith and that it has nothing to do with reality. There's a lot of confusion about faith both inside and outside the church. One of the most common assumptions is that faith is just a blind leap in the dark, that it's illogical and irrational and for superstitious people. Harvard professor of psychology Steven Pinker said the same thing but even more strongly: "Universities are about reason pure and simple. Faith—believing something without good reasons to do so—has no place in anything but a religious institution."[2]

Now, Pinker stacked the deck. I don't believe and I have never asked anyone to believe in something for which there were no "good reasons to do so." Neither the Bible nor Christianity asks anyone to exercise blind faith. Faith does not require you to check your brain at the door. If you exercise the right kind of faith in the right thing, you're not walking on eggshells or Jell-O. True faith is when you're standing on something you have strong reason to believe is true. Why? Because if you don't, that's not faith; it's presumption.

It's so important that you get this. Faith isn't believing something in spite of what you think is true; it's believing something because you have reason to believe it's true.

We all exercise that kind of faith every day. For example, you get on the internet to order something and enter your credit card number. Then you're sent a receipt. You don't have the product yet; it's not in your hands. But you have faith that it will arrive. All you have is a receipt, but you place your faith in that receipt.

When you make a reservation at a hotel, they give you a confirmation number. When you walk into the door of that hotel, you don't yet have a room, but you have faith that a room is reserved for you because of that confirmation number.

Faith in God is just as real as that kind of faith. It's just based on different evidence, which leads us to the word *assurance*. Also in verse 2, the author of Hebrews goes on to say that faith is "the assurance about what we don't see." The Greek word for "assurance" is a legal term that means "evidence" or "title-deed."[3] Faith is based on proof of things we can't even see.

So someone says, "See, you believe in something you can't see." But we all believe in things we've never seen—every day. Have you ever seen electricity? No, but I'll give you some advice: Don't stick your finger in a socket. Have you ever seen gravity? No, but I'll give you more advice: Don't jump off the Empire State Building without a parachute.

We live in two kinds of worlds—a world we can see and a world we can't see. For example, the podium I use to preach from is made up of atoms. You can't see those atoms; they're invisible to the naked eye. You can't see the electrons, protons, or neutrons bound together by electrical forces. What you can see is actually made of what you can't see. In fact, think about this: The reality of anything you can see right now was first an idea that you couldn't see.

That's exactly the way we see God—through the eyes of faith. Faith is the legal proof and the absolute assurance of things we can't see. I believe in an unseen God, for there's strong evidence that he is real and he is here. Which leads me to say...

## I BELIEVE IN A GOD WHO IS REAL

Hebrews 11:6 says, "Without faith it is impossible to please God." That's a thought-provoking statement. Think about it. No matter what you do or how well you do it, if you don't believe in God and place your faith in God it's impossible to please God. That means no matter how much money you give to the poor, how many times you attend church, or how many good works you do, you will never please God without faith in him.

Indeed, what else matters in life if you don't please God? If you please God, it doesn't matter whom you displease, and if you displease God, it doesn't matter whom you please.

Verse 6 goes on to say, "Anyone who comes to [God] must believe he exists." In order to please God, you've got to believe that he exists, that he's real. You have to believe that he's there even though you can't see him. You have to believe that God speaks even though you can't hear him. You must believe that God is with you even though you can't feel him. You must believe that God is near even though you can't touch him.

We have a saying: *Seeing is believing*. Well, it's also true that believing is seeing. In his book *PyroMarketing*, author Greg Steilstra tells about a fascinating study that involved a group of Americans who had never been to Mexico and a group of Mexicans who had never been to America. Researchers built a binocular viewing machine capable of showing one image to the right eye and one image to the left eye. One of the images was a baseball game and one of the images was a bullfight. During the test, the pictures appeared simultaneously, so the participants focused on one or the other. This is the fascinating thing: When asked what they'd seen, the Americans reported seeing a baseball game while the Mexicans reported seeing a bullfight.[4]

They discovered that on one level, seeing is believing. But on another level, believing is seeing. Oftentimes, what we see largely depends on what we expect or don't expect or what we want to see or don't want to see. In other words, we see what we're looking for.

These questions are raised, then: If God exists, why can't we see him? Why can't we hear him? Why can't we feel him? The thinking is, *I can believe in only what I can see, taste, touch, hear, or smell.* Again, that simply isn't true, and nobody lives that way. Can you see what you're thinking about right now? No. You can't see your thoughts. And a surgeon can see your brain, but he can't see your mind. You believe you have a mind. (If you don't believe you have a mind, you've lost your mind!) So if you can believe in things you can't see, why should you have a problem believing in a God you can't see?

I believe God has left his tracks in three ways: I believe he's left his tracks *naturally* in creation, I believe he's left his tracks *spiritually* in revelation (that is, in the Bible), and I believe he's left his tracks *physically* in the incarnation of Jesus Christ. So I don't deny that it takes faith to believe God exists, and I don't deny that it takes faith to believe that he created this world, but I also believe it takes a lot more faith to believe that everything we see and hear and taste and smell and touch got here by chance than to believe there's a God who created it. The truth is I don't have enough faith to be an atheist.

That's why only faith pleases God—because, frankly, you don't have to have faith in a God you can physically see. But you must have faith in a God you can spiritually see. Even when circumstances are tough, remember this: Doubt is putting your circumstances between you and God, but faith is putting God between you and your circumstances.

## I BELIEVE IN A
## GOD WHO IS RELIABLE

We've learned that the one thing that pleases God above all things is faith. Think about this—without faith, not only can you not please God, but if don't place your faith in him, you won't even please yourself. Have you considered that most of the problems in the life of believers occur because they don't believe? For example, you feel guilty when you don't believe in the grace of God, you worry when you don't believe in the goodness of God, and you disobey when you don't believe in the guidance of God.

That's why you need to understand the difference between the ordinary faith people exercise every day and the kind of God-faith we're talking about. Remember, the quality of faith depends upon the object in which you place your faith. You can have faith that water is fit to drink, but it could be poisoned. You can have faith that the brakes on your car work, but they might fail. You can have faith that you've paid for a product, but the check might bounce.

When you put your faith in God, you put your faith in a God who cannot lie, who cannot fail, who never changes, who never makes a mistake, and who always gets it right.

One surefire mark that you have real faith in the real God is that you pursue God believing that you'll find Him when you do. You see, a faith-filled heart is a following heart. One of the ways my eye doctor checks my eyes is by asking me to follow a light. When his light goes to the left, my eyes should shift to the left, and when his light goes to the right, my eyes should shift to the right. He knows that when my eyes are "right," they will follow the light.

If your heart is right, you will follow after God. You'll pursue God. You'll go after God. There's nothing wrong with possessing money, or a nice house, or lovely clothes, or a good job, or friendships, or things that bring us pleasure, but we should pursue only one thing: God. That's because Hebrews 11:6 tells us "he rewards those who earnestly seek him."

Here's the way it works: If you either look for a little of God or you look for him just a little, you'll get just a little of God. But the more of God you seek and the more you seek him, the more you'll find God and the more of him you'll find.

We Christians are too hard on atheists. Only one thing is worse than believing that God doesn't exist—not believing the God you say exists! I not only believe *in* God; I *believe* God!

———

What do you need to trust God with? Your finances? Your family? Your future? And yes, even your feelings? The God who sent his Son Jesus to die for us—the Son who was raised from the dead for us and who one day will come back for us—desires, demands, and deserves our faith. So come what may, every day in every way, say to the God who knows what he's doing and always does what's right, *I believe!* When you do, you'll find that your faith dictates your feelings. And when you know you're pleasing God, that's the greatest feeling of all!

# THE BEST RIDE

*We cannot cure the world of sorrows, but*
*we can choose to live in joy.*

**JOSEPH CAMPBELL**

Even if you're not into Mickey Mouse, there's no place on planet Earth like Disney World. As of this writing, it's still the most visited vacation resort in the world with an average attendance of 58 million visitors annually. All of the properties combined equal 27,258 acres (43 square miles), about the size of San Francisco and twice the size of Manhattan.

Each day guests wake up in one of the 30,000 hotel rooms, 409 wilderness cabins, and 799 campsites, and they're served by the nearly 70,000 cast members who are part of the Disney World staff. If guests get hungry, they can eat at one of more than 300 Disney restaurant outlets that, each year, serve 10 million hamburgers, 6 million hot dogs, 9 million pounds of French fries, 300,000 pounds of popcorn, 1.6 million turkey legs, 13 million bottles of water, and 75 million Coca-Colas.[1] Disney needs to sell a lot of these in order to make their annual budget, which is $59.4 billion dollars, roughly equal to the GDP of the entire nation of Croatia.[2]

Of course, you don't have to know any of these amazing facts to realize that Disney World is a special place. You only need to visit. I was there shortly after it opened in the 1971, when I was a sophomore at Stetson University in Florida. How could a college student afford to go to Disney World? Because then it cost only $3.50 to get in. I don't think that would buy me a hot dog anywhere on the property these days!

When you're there, you realize that what makes Disney World so special is not how big it is and not even how beautiful it is. The magic of Disney is how hard they work to accomplish the main purpose that inspired Walt Disney to build it in the first place. A recent article by an investigative reporter into what makes Disney World, Disney World, hit the bull's-eye with this statement: "Every last brick that holds up Disney World is built to *inspire joy* for children."[3] Disney wants every ride and every attraction's experience to bring joy. I can honestly say if you go to Disney World and don't experience some if not much joy, it's probably your own fault.

The problem is you can't take the joy of Disney World with you. When you leave Disney, you leave the Disney joy behind. But God never intended for life to be that way. With all of its troubles, headaches and heartaches, pain and suffering, God created this beautiful universe so that his children might have complete and consistent joy. That's why after Jesus said, "If you keep my commands, you will remain in my love, just as I have kept my Father's commands and remain in his love," he followed with, "I have told you this so that my joy may be in you and that your joy may be complete" (John 15:10-11).

You can't manufacture joy on your own, but it *is* a gift you can receive from God every day. I know you might think I'm crazy. You're sitting there thinking, *I can't* choose *joy*. But listen to John 15:11 again: "I have told you this so that my joy may be in you and that your joy may be complete."

Jesus is saying joy is a gift. He's saying, *I want to give you my joy so that your joy may be complete*. Did you know that every morning before you get out of bed you can pray this prayer? "Lord, today would you please give me your joy? And would you make my joy complete?" You can ask God for joy just like you can ask him for daily bread.

Perhaps you've heard of Joni Eareckson Tada. Joni is a quadriplegic. She dove into a lake at age 17, suffered a fracture between the fourth and fifth cervical vertebrae, and was instantly paralyzed from the shoulders down. In an article for *Decision* magazine, Joni told this story:

> Honesty is always the best policy when you are surrounded by women in a restroom during a break at a Christian women's conference. One woman, putting on lipstick, said, "Oh, Joni, you always look so together, so happy in your wheelchair. I wish I had your joy!" Several women around her nodded. "How do you do it?" she asked as she capped her lipstick.
>
> "I don't do it," I said. "May I tell you honestly how I woke up this morning? This is an average day. After my husband, Ken, leaves for work at 6:00 a.m., I'm alone until I hear the front door open at 7:00 a.m. That's when a friend arrives to get me up. While she makes coffee, I pray, 'Lord, my friend will soon give me a bath, get me dressed, set me up in my chair, brush my hair and teeth, and send me out the door. I don't have the strength to face this routine one more time. I have no resources. I don't have a smile to take into the day. May I have yours? God, I need you desperately.'"
>
> "So what happens when your friend comes into the bedroom?" one of them asked.
>
> "I turn my head toward her and give her a smile sent straight from heaven. It's not mine; it's God's." I point to

my paralyzed legs. "Whatever joy you see today was hard won this morning."[4]

Here's the hard truth: If you don't want to be joyful, you won't be. If you don't choose joy, you can't be joyful. And if you can't be joyful, you won't be joyful.

God wants all of us to live a life of joy. He wants life to be a joyride. We only get to take the ride of life once, so shouldn't it be the best ride? Even with the bumps in the road, the sharp curves, the steep cliffs, and the deep valleys, don't you want every hour of every day, of every week, of every year to be filled with joy? Would you like to face life every day with a smile on your face, a bounce to your step, and joy in your heart regardless of your circumstances? He wants joy to be a dominant feeling in our heart every day.

I understand that life isn't going well for some of you. You might even resent the fact that I'm calling you to be joyful. But we all have one thing in common: Nobody is immune to bad days. We all have them. You know it's going to be a bad day when...

- You call your answering service and they tell you it's none of your business.

- You put your pants on backward and they fit better.

- You see your best friend on "America's Most Wanted."

- Your two-year-old decides to finger paint your wall with peanut butter.

- You go to the bank to make a withdrawal and all the employees line up and start laughing at you.

- You arrive at the office and discover you're wearing two entirely different shoes.

- Your five-year-old rushes into your bedroom and says, "Did you know it's hard to flush a grapefruit down the toilet?'"

- You discover you're out of toilet paper—too late!

- You wake up in the middle of the night and realize your waterbed is broken—and then you remember you don't have a waterbed!

And some of us have bad weeks, bad months, and even bad years.

Well, Paul faced more than his share of bad times. In 2 Corinthians 11:24-28 he tells us he was given 39 lashes with a whip five times, he was beaten with rods three times, he was stoned once, and shipwrecked three times. He also survived a night and a day alone in the ocean, and he faced robbers, persecutors, and days without food and water. Yet he could still say, "Rejoice in the Lord always. I will say it again: Rejoice!" (Philippians 4:4).

This is really interesting. Before he wrote that, Paul even told the Philippians, "If you have any encouragement from being united with Christ, if any comfort from his love, if any common sharing in the Spirit, if any tenderness and compassion, then *make my joy complete by being like-minded*, having the same love, being one in spirit and of one mind" (Philippians 2:1-2, emphasis mine). Paul was saying his joy would not be complete until their joy was complete as well.

If you want to enjoy the ride of life, I guarantee you will if you'll just give Jesus preeminence, give others priority, and give yourself purpose.

## GIVE JESUS PREEMINENCE

Read Philippians 2:1-2 above again. What Paul says about rejoicing in the Lord in chapter 4 hinges on those two verses. You may not know this, but in the Greek language, this sentence doesn't indicate a possibility but a probability. The word *if* could be better translated "since" because it begins with our encouragement from being united with Christ.

In other words, Paul is assuming that the focal point of our lives will be Jesus. He will have first place, which means that nothing or no one surpasses Jesus in importance to us. Think about this. The fact that Jesus came to us, died for us, and lives in us to be with us through all eternity should bring you inexpressible, irrepressible joy.

Beyond that, we have the "comfort" from his love. It's not just that Jesus lives in us; he loves us. And it's because he loves us that we love him. Think about the added benefit to that. If I love Jesus and you love Jesus, then we're going to love each other. Do you understand why that's so important for us? Why we exist? To point people to Jesus and inspire them to follow him completely. Do you know the number one way we point people to Jesus? By loving one another. Jesus said, "By this everyone will know that you are my disciples, if you love one another" (John 13:35).

When people sense that we truly love one another, then they'll know we truly love Jesus. That's when they'll see the difference following Jesus makes.

The way we give Jesus preeminence, keeping him first, is as Paul said, through the "common sharing in the Spirit." Now, that phrase *common sharing* means to share in common. It's the Spirit's job to keep us focused on Jesus, to keep us in love with Jesus, to keep us pointing people to Jesus, and to keep our minds and hearts on Jesus. But that raises a question. If the Holy Spirit lives in every Christian, why do Christians sometimes fight and divide and don't get along?

That happens because there's a difference between the indwelling of the Holy Spirit and the influence of the Holy Spirit. You see, every believer is equally indwelt by the Holy Spirit, but not every believer is equally influenced by the Holy Spirit.

When we get out of fellowship with the Holy Spirit, guess what? We get out of fellowship with one another. Think about it this way: You can't pit the Holy Spirit against the Holy Spirit. He will not fight himself. You can't divide the Holy Spirit. As long as I'm full of the Holy Spirit and in fellowship with the Holy Spirit and you're full of the Holy Spirit and in fellowship with the Holy Spirit, we can disagree, debate, and discuss, but we can't divide unless it's over a vital biblical belief or principle we can't compromise on.

And as we noted, Paul goes on to say, "Make my joy complete by being like-minded" (verse 2). To be like-minded doesn't mean we'll always think the same way, but it does mean we'll think on the same things. Thinking the same way means we all agree that we should give Jesus preeminence in our lives, but that doesn't mean we'll always think the same thing. It doesn't mean we'll all see things the same way. There's nothing wrong with having differences and discussions and debates and even disagreements. But it does mean we'll never let politics, preferences, or personalities divide us. Paul says that will result in our "having the same love, being one in spirit and of one mind" (Philippians 2:2).

If I love Jesus supremely and you love Jesus supremely, then we will love each other. When you're hitting on all eight cylinders with the Son of God, the love of God, and the Spirit of God, you'll be full of joy.

## GIVE OTHERS PRIORITY

How do you know you have given Jesus preeminence? How do you know he is truly in first place? Well, there's a sure tell sign: You put others second. That doesn't come naturally, however; it comes supernaturally. The first thing you have to do is die to selfishness. That's why Paul next said, "Do nothing out of selfish ambition or vain conceit" (Philippians 2:3).

Selfish ambition is when you seek to put others down, and conceit is when you seek to build yourself up. Selfish ambition is when you want to win even if everybody else loses. Conceit is when you believe you deserve to win and everybody else deserves to lose.

This is so difficult to deal with because we're all born this way. Think about it. You have to teach a child not to be selfish. Do you know what children's favorite words are when they first learn to talk? *Me, my,* and *mine.* "Give it to me. That toy is mine. My doll." One of the first lessons you have to teach a child is how to think of others first. The problem is we're born with the desire to put ourselves first.

I love the story of the young mother who was preparing pancakes for her two sons, Kevin, five, and Ryan, three. The boys began to argue over who should get the first pancake. This mother saw an opportunity for a teachable moment and said, "Now, boys, if Jesus was sitting here, he would say, 'Let my brother have the first pancake. I can wait.'"

Kevin turned to his younger brother and said, "Ryan, you be Jesus."[5]

Let's face it. We all want everybody else to be Jesus. But there's only one antidote to selfishness, only one way you will put others second and yourself third, and here it is from Paul: "In humility value others above yourselves" (Philippians 2:3).

Instead of running over each other trying to be first, we ought to be falling over each other trying to be second. I know that's counterintuitive and countercultural. But the way to joy is to look out for others. We're told to do everything possible to get ahead, but God says to do everything possible to get behind. We're told, *If you have to, step on other people to get to the top.* God says, *Put other people on your shoulders to help them get to the top.* I bet you've had the same experience I've had: I've never met a joyful person who was selfish and always put themselves first.

The way to joy is to think of others the way you ought to think of others and think of you the way you ought to think of you. How do you do that? Always value others as more important than yourself. That word *value* refers to a conclusion that's carefully thought out based on what is true. You don't just pretend that others are more important than you are; you've got to actually believe that others are more important than you are. And if you're looking accurately, you will.

In a letter to the Romans, Paul wrote, "By the grace given me I say to every one of you: Do not think of yourself more highly than you ought, but rather think of yourself with sober judgment" (Romans 12:3). You know what's true of all of us at some point in our lives? We really do think more highly of ourselves than we think of others.

The late Don Shula was the head coach of the Miami Dolphins and the only coach who ever won a Super Bowl with an undefeated team. This is a story about Shula reported around the time he was inducted into the Pro Football Hall of Fame:

> After he coached the 1972 Miami Dolphins to a 17-0 record, he and his late wife, Dorothy, vacationed in a small town on the Maine coast. Entering a movie theater one evening, they received a standing ovation. "You don't have to applaud," Shula said. "I don't want any special treatment, even if my team did just win the Super Bowl."
>
> From the back of the dark theater came a voice. "We don't care who you are," it said. "They wouldn't start the movie until we had 10 people here. You and your wife put us over the top."[6]

Don't think too highly of yourself and think more highly of others. That raises a question. *If I'm going to think everybody else is more important than I am, then who's going to think I'm important?* Well, when you think it over, you'll reach the same conclusion someone else did: "If I think you're more important than I am…and you think I'm more important than you are…and he thinks she's more important than he is…and she thinks he's more important than she is…then in the end everyone feels important but no one acts important."

Joy comes from giving others priority.

## GIVE YOURSELF PURPOSE

In verse 4 Paul completes his admonition with "not looking to your own interests but each of you to the interests of the others" (Philippians 2:4). No one who has ever lived was more full of joy than Jesus. No one who has ever lived gave out more joy than Jesus. His life was pure, unadulterated, undiluted, undeniable joy because from the moment he came to this planet to the moment he left it he was looking out for our interests, not his own.

Do you know what purpose will get you where you want to go in life? Not just putting others second and yourself third but actually helping others get where they want to go in life.

My late friend Zig Ziglar used to put it this way: "You can have everything in life you want, if you will just help other people get what they want."[7] Let me stop and answer the question you're probably asking. *If I look out for others, who will look out for me?* Let me share a principle that's also a promise: When you look out for others, God will look out for you.

A strange law in the kingdom of God works like this: The lower you get, the higher you go. So the secret to joy is not being able to climb to the top of the ladder; it's being willing to go to the lowest rung and give a helping hand up. In his book *Thinking for a Change*, John C. Maxwell stated, "There is no life as empty as a self-centered life. There is no life so centered as a self-empty life."[8]

Now do you realize that giving Jesus first place, others second place, and yourself third place is what will give you the most pleasure? Let me put together these three points, and I think you'll see what I mean.

Give **J**esus preeminence.

Give **O**thers priority.

Give **Y**ourself purpose.

Does that look familiar? Doing those three things will give you the best ride of all—joy. It's the ride God designed life to be.

# THANK YOU VERY MUCH

*Gratitude is a currency that we can mint for ourselves
and spend without fear of bankruptcy.*

**FRED DE WITT VAN AMBURGH**

At the turn of the nineteenth century and into the early twentieth century, British writer Rudyard Kipling was at the peak of his career and one of the most widely read men in the world. He won a Nobel Prize for literature, and his children's Jungle Book series is still widely read today. His literary work also made him a great deal of money. Here's a story about that:

> At the height of his popularity, a newspaper reporter approached him and said, "Mr. Kipling, I just read that somebody calculated that the money you make from your writings amounts to over $100 a word."
>
> Mr. Kipling raised his eyebrows and said, "Really, I certainly wasn't aware of that."
>
> The reporter cynically reached into his pocket and pulled out a $100 bill, gave it to Kipling and said, "Here's a $100

bill, Mr. Kipling. Now you give me one of your $100 words."

Kipling looked at the $100 bill for a moment, took it, folded it up, put it in his pocket and then said, "Thanks."[1]

That word *thanks* may have been a hundred-dollar word a century or two ago, but I would say today it's more like a million-dollar word. Today it's too rarely spoken, too rarely heard, and too often forgotten. It seems like we live in an ocean of ingratitude and walk in a desert of gratitude.

I couldn't believe my eyes when I read that a 27-year-old man in India had sued his parents for "creating him"[2] and that he "told the BBC that it's wrong to bring children into the world because they then have to put up with lifelong suffering."[3] By the way, I think his chances in court were pretty slim since both of his parents were attorneys!

We all carry and experience various emotions, and feelings matter. So many of us too often don't do what we think we should do but what we feel we should do. Although you can't necessarily choose how you feel, you can choose your attitude, and attitude determines altitude. One of the greatest antidotes to negative feelings and emotions is the attitude of gratitude.

Our being thankful is so important to God that he actually commands us to be thankful. Paul went through a tremendous amount of suffering and heartache that would cause anybody to be bitter and ungrateful and maybe even mad at God. You may not *feel* thankful right now because of where you are in your life, but you can *be* thankful.

In 1 Thessalonians 5, Paul tells us not only why we should be thankful but how we should be thankful: habitually, happily and generously, and humbly.

## BE HABITUALLY THANKFUL

We all know we should be thankful at least for certain things at certain times, but what Paul says may shock your system: "Give thanks in all circumstances" (1 Thessalonians 5:18).

In the Greek language that means "in all things,"[4] which makes this verse difficult for all of us. If Paul had said, "Give thanks in most circumstances" or "most of the time," we could live with that. Most people want to thank God in "good circumstances," and we certainly could live with that. But Paul said we're to give thanks in all things at all times.

Since we're talking about feelings, let me give you a word of caution. Nowhere in Scripture will you find a command to "feel" thankful. Feelings come and feelings go. Feelings can be affected by the weather, by the temperature, by the functioning of your liver, by how much rest you got the night before, or by how the stock market is doing. Giving thanks has nothing to do with feelings. You can be thankful even if you don't feel thankful. Whether things are good or bad, we're to give thanks.

Giving thanks is a big deal to God. One of the sacrifices Israel was instructed to make on a regular basis was the "thank offering" or "peace offering." It was designed to remind them of their need to be thankful. They were to bring a sheaf of grain or some oil and wine as an offering of thanksgiving to acknowledge that God always provided for their needs and to remember they were to always be grateful for what he had done for them even though their experiences hadn't all been smooth sailing.

Paul says we're to give thanks *in* "all circumstances," not necessarily *for* all circumstances. We may not be thankful for trouble, but we are to be thankful in the midst of trouble.

Do you know one of the reasons God allows bad things to happen to us? He wants to move us to thanksgiving! In a letter to the Corinthians, Paul wrote about all the difficult things Christians experience, from oppression to persecution to death. Then he said, "All this is for your benefit, so that the grace that is reaching more and more people may cause thanksgiving to overflow to the glory of God" (2 Corinthians 4:15).

In his book *Money, Possessions, and Eternity,* Randy Alcorn tells this story about two real-life men:

> In America, a sharp-looking businessman stands up at a luncheon to give his testimony: "Before I knew Christ, I had nothing. My business was in bankruptcy, my health was ruined, I'd lost the respect of the community, and I'd almost lost my family. Then I accepted Christ. He took me out of bankruptcy and now my business has tripled its profits. My blood pressure has dropped to normal, and I feel better than I've felt in years. Best of all, my wife and children have come back, and we're a family again. God is so good—praise the Lord!"
>
> In China, a disheveled former university professor gives his testimony: "Before I met Christ, I had everything. I made a large salary, lived in a nice house, enjoyed good health, was highly respected for my credentials and profession, and had a good marriage and a beautiful son. Then I accepted Christ as my Savior and Lord. As a result, I lost my post at the university, lost my beautiful house and car, and spent five years in prison. Now I work for a subsistence wage at a factory. I live with pain from my neck, which was broken in prison. My wife rejected me because of my conversion. She took my son away, and I haven't seen him for ten years. But God is good, and I praise him for his faithfulness."
>
> Both men are sincere Christians. One gives thanks because of what he's gained. The other gives thanks in spite of what he's lost.[5]

If God is sovereign and God is good, then everything that happens *to* you also happens *for* you, and that's why you're to give thanks in every situation. Regardless of how bad it may seem to you, God wants to use it to grow you and move you to thanksgiving.

## BE HAPPILY AND GENEROUSLY THANKFUL

I've learned that anything God commands me to do is for my best and for my benefit. And because of that, I truly believe that a grateful person will be a happier person, a holier person, and a healthier person.

Many well-substantiated medical studies have found that gratitude increases patience, decreases depression, replenishes willpower, and reduces stress.[6] It doesn't just make your life longer; it makes your life better. In 2010, Robert Emmons, said to be the leading expert on gratitude, reported:

> We've studied more than one thousand people, from ages eight to 80, and found that people who practice gratitude consistently report a host of benefits:
>
> **Physical**
>
> - Stronger immune systems
> - Less bothered by aches and pains
> - Lower blood pressure
> - Exercise more and take better care of their health
> - Sleep longer and feel more refreshed upon waking
>
> **Psychological**
>
> - Higher levels of positive emotions
> - More alert, alive, and awake

- More joy and pleasure

- More optimism and happiness

**Social**

- More helpful, generous, and compassionate

- More forgiving

- More outgoing

- Feel less lonely and isolated[7]

Mark Batterson gave this advice in his book *Double Blessing*: "If you want a good night's sleep, don't count sheep. Count your blessings!"[8]

But to give thanks is not just good advice; it's a divine command. Gratitude is not an option; it's an obligation. You're just as obligated to give God your thanks as you are to give him your time. In other words, it's a sin to be ungrateful.

When you give something to someone, it's usually because they need it, they deserve it, or they want it. If you don't give it to them, you rob them of the blessing. There's no greater way you can bless someone, whether God or another human being, than to express your thanks to them. For example,

- Have you ever thanked your mom and dad for bringing you into this world?

- Have you ever thanked the person who led you to Christ?

- Have you ever thanked the coach or teacher who helped you turn from the wrong path to the right path?

- Have you ever thanked a police officer, a firefighter, or any first responder for the service they give to the public?

How about everything you experience and enjoy each day but don't even think about? I don't know how long ago the following statistics were put together, but you'll get the point, and maybe they'll help you push your thanksgiving button.

- "If you woke up this morning with more health than illness, you are more blessed than the million who will not survive this week.

- If you have never experienced the danger of battle, the loneliness of imprisonment, the agony of torture or the pangs of starvation, you are ahead of 500 million people around the world.

- If you attend a church meeting without fear of harassment, arrest or torture of death, you are more blessed than almost three billion people in the world.

- If you have food in your refrigerator, clothes on your back, a roof over your head and a place to sleep, you are richer than 75% of the world.

- If you have money in the bank, in your wallet, and spare change in a dish someplace, you are among the top 8% of the world's wealthy...

- If you can read this message, you are more blessed than over two billion people in the world that cannot read anything at all."[9]

You may not always feel thankful, but you should work harder to think about saying *Thank you*. It's better to say *thank you* and not mean it than to mean it and not say it.

In his book *What Losing Taught Me About Winning*, Fran Tarkenton, the great University of Georgia quarterback who played for the Minnesota Vikings, tells about how he once blocked a running back in a tight Vikings game. The play went well, and they eventually scored a touchdown.

To make a point about the importance of sharing the rewards of hard work, Tarkenton told what happened the next day when his coach, Bud Grant, met with the team: "When Bud got to the key play, he slowed the film and carefully and incisively broke down every aspect of it, praising the near-perfect execution and noting the role of every player."

But Grant didn't even mention Tarkenton, and after the meeting, Tarkenton asked him about it. Grant admitted Tarkenton's block had been great, but then said, "Fran, you are such a self-starter, such a highly motivated and positive guy, I didn't think I needed to say anything to you in front of the other guys. Should I?"

What did Tarkenton honestly reply? He said if his coach ever wanted to see him block again, he better thank him![10]

We should be happily and generously thankful.

## BE HUMBLY THANKFUL

Paul tells us the greatest reason we should give thanks: "For this is God's will for you in Christ Jesus" (1 Thessalonians 5:18).

I don't know what you're going through right now or what burdens you may be bearing or what trouble you might be in, but if you're completely ungrateful without an ounce of gratitude in your heart even in the midst of your circumstances, you're out of the will of God.

Now, be encouraged. When Paul says this is the will of God, he's not only saying this is what God desires for you to do but that it's what God enables you to do. God never commands us to do anything he doesn't give us the power to do. I know I can give thanks in all things.

Why? Because it's God's will, and what God wants me to do and wills me to do, he enables me to do.

Remember, God's will for you is always what's best for you. An attitude of gratitude will change your life. It will shield you from cynicism. It will keep you from criticism. It will protect you from pessimism. It will draw you close to God and draw God close to you. If you have a heart for God, you will have a grateful heart, and that will change how you see things. In fact, one of the greatest ways to change how you feel about things is to change the way you see things.

Let me ask you a question. If you were competing in the Olympics for a medal, would you rather win the silver medal or the bronze medal? A study of Olympic medal winners produced some unexpected results. Most people would assume that the silver medal winners would be happier than the bronze medal winners since they received the higher honor, but that wasn't the case. Believe it or not, the bronze medalists who came in third place seemed happier than the silver medalists who finished in second place. Why? A behavioral scientist explains, "For silver, you think, 'Oh, I could have won the gold,' and for bronze, it's 'At least I got a medal.'"[11]

What happens to you is not nearly as important as how you perceive what happens to you. It all depends on your perspective.

- I can complain because it's raining, or I can be thankful that the grass is being watered for free.

- I can complain because roses have thorns, or I can be thankful that thorns have roses.

- I can whine because I have to go to work, or I can be thankful that I have a job.

- I can gripe because I've got to do housework, or I can be thankful I have a house to work in.

- I can grieve over the failures of my parents, or I can be thankful they allowed me to be born.

- I can choose to be grumbly hateful, or I can choose to be humbly grateful.

I want to be like the 98-year-old woman who was lying on her deathbed, her grandson at her side. She'd been asleep for a while when, suddenly, she woke up and said, "I'm so thankful."

Her grandson said, "Granny, what are you thankful for?"

"I only have two teeth, but thank God they meet!"

My prayer is that of William Shakespeare, the greatest dramatist and writer in the English language of all time: "O Lord that lends me life, lend me a heart replete with thankfulness."[12]

When Abraham Lincoln was president, he started an unusual Thanksgiving tradition that every president since then has followed. The Wednesday before Thanksgiving he pardoned a turkey. Following his tradition, the turkey is now brought into the Rose Garden, where the commander-in-chief, the most powerful person in the world, grants that big bird a pardon. That turkey is then taken to a Virginia farm where it's granted immunity and lives until it has a natural death.

Now, that brings a smile to our faces, but it's also a great reminder that without Jesus we are all turkeys headed to slaughter. Because of the grace of God, the Son of God, the love of God, the mercy of God, and the salvation of God, we can be granted spiritual immunity free of sin and enjoy eternal life. That's why every day is thanksgiving day and we should look up to this wonderful God and say to him, *Thank you very much!*

# TOTALLY SATISFIED

*He who is not contented with what he has, would not
be contented with what he would like to have.*

**SOCRATES**

When Peter McGinnis was a student at Harvard Business School in the early 2000s, he penned a column for the student newspaper that would add to the English language. In his article, McGinnis argued "that the student body's social schedules were driven by two forces."[1] One of them was what McGinnis called "the Fear of Missing Out."

FOMO for short, it went viral, and its definition was eventually included in the *Oxford English Dictionary*: "fear of missing out: anxiety that an exciting or interesting event may be happening elsewhere, often aroused by posts seen on a social media website."[2]

So FOMO is basically the feeling of fear induced by the *potential* of regret. People who struggle with FOMO may not know exactly what they're missing out on, but they assume that other people are having a more entertaining or rewarding life experience.

The older I get, the more I wrestle with this fear. I want to be included and invited, and when I'm not, my sense of satisfaction with life can quietly erode. This is compounded by the fact that the most important thing many people want in life is satisfaction.

In their book *Renovation of the Church*, authors Kent Carlson and Mike Lueken tell us,

> Getting what we want is part of daily life in our culture. If we don't like a television show, we hit the button. If we don't like this song…we hit the button. If the church stops meeting our needs, we hit the button. Every day we are told that what we have is insufficient. We are bombarded with messages urging us to upgrade, trade in or borrow to buy. Our economy thrives on perpetual discontent. The long-term consequence of this relentless marketing of dissatisfaction is that we become accustomed to having our needs met when and how we want. We become experts at "dissatisfaction remediation."[3]

One of the first words children learn to say is *more*. It takes a long time for them to learn to say the word *enough*. Maybe it's not coincidental that the song *Rolling Stone Magazine* ranks as the number two song in its 500 greatest songs of all time and the number one song on VH-1's 100 Greatest Rock Songs of all time is "(I Can't Get No) Satisfaction."[4,5] It seems that discontent and dissatisfaction follow us throughout life.

We spend most of our lives working, and we spend most of our time working at a job we're dissatisfied with. In 2019, *Staff Squared HR* reported this: "A global poll conducted by Gallup has uncovered that out of the world's one billion full-time workers, only 15% of people are engaged at work. That means that an astronomical 85% of people are unhappy in their jobs."[6]

Although we didn't cover it in Part One of this book, discontentment can block the light of joy, peace, and happiness even at high noon.

Given all of this, it's hard to imagine a world where we can feel totally satisfied. But according to that ancient Jewish missionary named Paul, the road to contentment is available to us all if only we'll remember God's purpose for us, rely on his power in us, and rest in his provision for us.

## REMEMBER GOD'S PURPOSE FOR YOU

As we said earlier, Philippians was penned by the apostle Paul, who wrote it from a Roman prison while he was literally "chained to his desk." If anyone had a reason to gripe and complain, it was Paul. But instead, he decided to reflect on the transformative power of contentment:

> I rejoiced greatly in the Lord that at last you renewed your concern for me. Indeed, you were concerned, but you had no opportunity to show it. I am not saying this because I am in need, for I have learned to be content whatever the circumstances. I know what it is to be in need, and I know what it is to have plenty. I have learned the secret of being content in any and every situation, whether well fed or hungry, whether living in plenty or in want (Philippians 4:10-12).

Paul is commending this church in Philippi because they had done all they could to meet his needs while he was in that prison. But at the end of the day, he was still imprisoned, and that's a pretty good excuse for feeling discontented. He had been unfairly treated, unlovingly rejected, unjustly imprisoned. The Jewish people who once adored him now hated him because he'd given his life to Christ. He was imprisoned because they'd unfairly convicted him of a crime he didn't commit.

Yet even with the dark cloud of death hanging over him, God's presence anchored Paul in inexplicable contentment. He'd still learned to stave off the dissatisfaction that most of us would feel in that situation and instead cultivate joy in the imperfections of the present moment.

If you can be totally satisfied in prison, surely you can be totally satisfied outside of one!

There's a secret to satisfaction, and Paul said he'd *learned* it. You see, contentment isn't just a principle you practice; it's a lesson you learn. A school from which you never graduate, never earn a doctorate, never get a summer break or Christmas vacation is God's school of lifelong learning. When you give your heart to God, you enroll in his university, and he teaches every class. The word *disciple* means "learner."[7] God never quits teaching, and we should never quit learning. School is never out.

It doesn't matter what you're doing. Whether you're reading your Bible, facing a problem, parenting a child, working in a difficult job, going through a tough time, or dealing with a medical issue, you should always be asking, *God, what do you want to teach me?* And one of the greatest lessons God wants to teach us is how to be content.

Even in that rat-infested, dank, dark, cold prison, what had Paul learned? He'd learned how to be satisfied when times were good and when times were bad. He'd learned to be satisfied in abundance and in lack. He learned to be satisfied when he was going with the flow or forced to swim upstream. And that enabled him to be completely content and totally satisfied even there.

Here's the secret: Contentment is realizing you don't have to control everything because God's in control of everything. It means accepting that you're not under your circumstances and that God is over your circumstances. Paul didn't know what was going to happen to him, but he knew God did. Paul didn't know whether he would have a little or a lot, but he knew he had God. If you have everything without God, you have nothing. But if you have nothing with God, you have everything.

That's why the most dissatisfied, discontented, dysfunctional people can become control freaks. But we can't control everything. Paul had made up his mind he was going to be satisfied with who he was, with where he was, with what he had, and with the God who was sovereign over all of those things. You don't have to keep up with the Joneses if can learn to be satisfied being a Smith!

I love the old story about a king who longed for contentment. He just couldn't find inner peace. One of his advisers suggested they search for a contented man and bring back that man's shirt. Then the king could put it on and be content as well. The king sent them out, and they searched all over the kingdom for the most satisfied, contented man they could find. But when they found him, he didn't even own a shirt!

You see, contentment is an acquired skill. You can learn to be satisfied with who you are, where you are, and what you have, and that's exactly what God wants to teach you.

God's plan for you is to be satisfied in him, his purpose for you is to glorify him, and the latter is impossible without the former.

## RELY ON GOD'S POWER IN YOU

A few years ago, my middle son, Jonathan, decided to go on a pilgrimage of sorts. He took a break from the rat race and traveled to the New Mexico desert. There he found a Trappist monastery that's completely off the grid. He checked in, and the abbot showed him to a simple room with no television, no internet access, one tiny window, a slouching twin-size bed, and a Bible. The monk said, "I hope you enjoy your stay, and if you need anything, please let us know. We're happy to teach you how to live without it."

That may sound unrealistic or even extreme depending on the hand you've been dealt. You may assume there's no way you could be satisfied with where you are or what you have or how you look. And in one sense, you're right. On your own, you can't.

That's why Paul adds, "I can do all this through him who gives me strength" (Philippians 4:13). This may be one of the most misunderstood verses in the Bible, because Paul was not saying "I can do anything I want to do." He was saying, "I can be totally satisfied with who I am, where I am, and what I have because I have the power to do it through Christ." We can do or be anything God wants us to do or be, and God wants us to be totally satisfied.

We are called to contentment, but it will never come when you reach the top of the ladder, build a fat bank account, or gain that title you've always been looking for. It comes when you change the way you think and rely on the power God has given you.

I love the cartoon strip *Peanuts*, and in one strip Snoopy is in his doghouse on Thanksgiving. He's grumbling about being stuck with dog food while everybody else is inside eating turkey and gravy, dressing, cranberries, and pumpkin pie. Then he thinks to himself, *It might have been worse...I might have been born a turkey!*[8]

How would your life look different if you stopped griping about what you *don't* have and started nurturing gratitude for what you *do* have?

How would your life look different if you stopped complaining about where you *aren't* and started nurturing contentment with where you *are*?

How would your life look different if you stopped sulking about who you *aren't* and nurtured satisfaction about who you *are*?

Many of us would realize we're already ahead. You see, we all think we can't do a lot of things we can. You need to remember this about the life you live as a follower of Jesus: The Christian life is not a matter of can or can't; it's a matter of will or won't. God doesn't just command you to do something; he enables you to do it. If you know what God wants you to do, he's already given you the power to do it.

God has a purpose for you—to find your total satisfaction in him. He's put his power in you, enabling you to overcome FOMO, greed, materialism, selfishness, and the desire to always get ahead and have more. Focus on him every day and realize that if you're living for him, you're where you're supposed to be and you're who you're supposed to be.

You'll also have everything you need.

## REST IN GOD'S PROVISION FOR YOU

God makes some great promises in his Word, but I don't know of a greater promise than the one Paul gives next: "My God will meet all your needs according to the riches of his glory in Christ Jesus" (Philippians 4:19). Think about the big idea Paul is giving us here: If you're living in the center of God's will, you can rest knowing that God will meet any real need in your life.

It's been said many times, but it's worth saying again: God has promised to supply our need but not our greed. He's never promised to give us everything we want and wish for. He's not a heavenly waiter whose job it is to attend to our every desire. And that's actually good news. I've lived long enough to be thankful God hasn't given me everything I've ever wanted.

But I'm also thankful he's given me everything I've needed even when I didn't want it. Just like all kids, sometimes I needed to be disciplined, but I certainly wasn't mature enough to find my father and say, "Dad, do you have a minute? I need some discipline." Yet I'm thankful my parents cared enough about me to provide discipline when I wasn't the kind of person I should have been.

On the other hand, too often we want things we really don't need. I almost married the wrong girl twice, and I'm so grateful that God didn't give me the ones I wanted but the one I needed. Not a day goes by that I'm not grateful to God that I married Teresa. She doesn't give me everything I want, but she gives me everything I need.

Sometimes we want flattery, but what we need is honesty. When I turned 50, it was a traumatic time for me. I'd been kind of walking around the house depressed, when finally, I walked into our bedroom and said, "Teresa, you don't think I look 50, do you?"

She said, "No. But you used to!"

God's promise has never failed. His word has never been broken. If you have a real need in your life, God will meet it. But if he hasn't met that need yet, one of two things is true: Either your need is not a true need or you don't need it yet. And even a true need may not be met in your way and in your time, but it will be in his. God will provide. In fact, when you realize he already has in many ways, contentment will be yours.

———

Here's a story that illustrates something about contentment via an unhappy farmer:

> The farmer complained about the lake on his property that always needed to have the fish thinned out. The rolling hills made it more difficult for him to run the fence rows. Sometimes he couldn't even see his cows because they had so much territory to cover. At night it was so dark it was hard to walk from the barn back to his house.
>
> He decided to sell the place and move somewhere really nice. He called a real estate agent and made plans to sell his property.

A few days later he picked up the local paper, looking for a new place to live. His eye caught an ad for a lovely country home in an ideal location—quiet and peaceful.

It had soft rolling hills…a pristine lake stocked with bass, a classic barn surrounded by natural flowers and soft grass, and came complete with a wonderful herd of Black Angus cows. It was just close enough to a small town to be convenient but far enough out to be uncluttered by city lights, traffic and noise.

He read the ad a second and then a third time before realizing the real estate agent had given her description of the place he currently owned. He called her and told her to cancel the ad. He said, "I've changed my mind. I've been looking for a place like that all my life."[9]

The next time you feel a pinch of FOMO and want to know how to deal with how you feel, stop looking around and start looking up. Take a moment to remember God's purpose for you, rely on his power in you, and rest in his provision. This is the road to contentment and the path to total satisfaction.

# THE ONLY TRUE SOURCE

*We must accept finite disappointment,
but never lose infinite hope.*

**MARTIN LUTHER KING JR.**

We've all come to know a word most of us had never heard of when 2020 rolled around. It's known worldwide, and it's a word we'll never forget even though we'd like to. That word is *coronavirus*. Since almost no one was old enough to remember the 1918 Spanish influenza pandemic, we'd never seen anything like COVID-19. I heard my parents talk many times about the Great Depression, but they never went through the social, personal, and commercial isolation this disease brought. At least during the Depression, people could go out even if they couldn't work. In the early days of COVID-19, almost no one but essential workers could safely go out at all.

When circumstances drive emotions into the ground, people honestly aren't looking for some *Rah, rah, go get 'em* speech or positive thinking platitudes. To be even more blunt, as a pastor I realize people want more than just another sermon. What they're looking for, hungry for, begging for, thirsting for, living for, and even dying for is *hope*.

Hope isn't only one of the most powerful words in the English language; it's truly one of the most powerful forces in the world.

In his book *Developing the Leaders Around You,* John C. Maxwell shares this story: "Winston Churchill recognized the power of hope. He was prime minister of England during some of the darkest hours of World War II. He was once asked by a reporter what his country's great weapon had been against Hitler's Nazi regime. Without pausing for a moment he said, 'It was what England's greatest weapon has always been—hope.'"[1]

I want to put my cards on the table up front. I believe that the one day of the year people all over the globe celebrate the greatest event in the history of the world—the resurrection of Jesus—represents not only the hope for all mankind that life can have a happy ending as well as a purposeful existence but represents our only true hope. Why do I make such an audacious claim? Because if the message of Easter is true, if Jesus is alive, if he was raised from the dead, then not only do we have hope, and not only do we have the best hope, but we have the only hope for our past, our present, and our future. Only a risen Lord can take care of yesterday, today, and tomorrow. Those of us who believe in a risen Lord may feel helpless, but we're never hopeless. As believers, we have a sure hope.

Peter literally gave his life for what he believed in and preached until his last breath—the resurrection of Jesus. He'd seen the risen Savior with his own eyes. But before he died, he wrote a letter found in the New Testament, called 1 Peter. In chapter 1 he says why Jesus' resurrection gives the entire world hope in any situation: God gives us spiritual life, God guards us in our personal lives, and God guides us to eternal life.

## GOD GIVES US SPIRITUAL LIFE

In 1 Peter, Peter is writing to a group of Christians throughout various regions who are under tremendous persecution for their faith.

They're being imprisoned. They're being beaten. They're being crucified. According to church tradition, Peter himself was eventually crucified—upside down.

Peter writes these great words: "Praise be to the God and Father of our Lord Jesus Christ! In his great mercy he has given us new birth into a living hope through the resurrection of Jesus Christ from the dead" (1 Peter 1:3).

Because Jesus was raised from the dead, we have what Peter calls "a living hope." It's not an ordinary hope, like *I hope to win the lottery*, or *I hope to get a date with that cheerleader*, or *I hope I aced that test even though I didn't study*. That's just wishful thinking. I read about a second-grade teacher who was teaching her class some vocabulary. She said, "What is the definition of hope?" One of her students said, "Hope is wishing for something you know ain't going to happen."

But Peter is talking about a living hope that never dies and can never fail. We're told that's true because the greatest hope anybody could ever have is the hope that there's life after death, the hope that there's more to this life than this life. It's the hope we all need.

The U.S. Air Force trains its soldiers to memorize two numbers to help them survive trauma. One is the optimum body temperature, 98.6, and the other is the number 3. One of the things they say soldiers might not achieve survival without—as well as without air, shelter, food, water, and companionship in a certain amount of time—is "3 seconds without spirit and hope."[2]

Peter tells us we have a hope that will never die. Why? Because through that resurrection and faith in the risen Lord, we have a new birth, a new beginning, a new life. That means the moment you're born again your lifelong slate is wiped clean. Past sins and even present and future sins are under God's forgiveness. Every human being was meant to have two births. We were born physically, but we must be born again spiritually. We were born once, but we're meant to be born twice. The first birth places us into a human family. The second birth places us into a heavenly family.

And this new birth is given to us once and for all. How many times do you have to be born physically? Once. How many times do you have to be born again, this time spiritually? Once. Once you're born again, you never have to be born again. Do you realize the hope that ought to give you?

When you're born again, three things occur:

1. God forgives your sin.

2. God adopts you into his family.

3. God becomes your Father.

We can trust God for today and tomorrow because he changes our life yesterday. Believers don't have to worry about the past because God has given us spiritual life.

Now, the question you should ask yourself right about now is this: *Has God given me that spiritual life? Have I been born again? Or have I been born only once?* You had better be born twice, because if not, one day you'll wish you had never been born at all.

Next, because of the resurrection, we have a sure hope for our present.

## GOD GUARDS US IN OUR PERSONAL LIVES

The moment we receive spiritual life—that new birth and that new beginning—God takes over. This is what Peter says God does because of our faith: We are "shielded by God's power until the coming of the salvation that is ready to be revealed in the last time" (1 Peter 1:5).

*Shielded* is a military term. It means to be guarded by a garrison of soldiers, and the believer is guarded by God's power. What kind of power is Peter talking about? The power that God used to raise Jesus from the dead. And that same power God used to bring Jesus' body back to life is the power that guards our bodies in this life. That's the power that keeps us safe and secure.

If you ever doubt God's power to protect you, just think about the power that raised Jesus from the dead. There's no greater power than resurrection power. The greatest power human beings possess on their own is the power to kill, but the power to raise someone from the dead is even greater than that. Those of us who have placed our faith in the risen Lord are under heaven's lock and key, protected by the most efficient security system available in all of the universe. We live under the protection of God every day, and most of us don't even realize it.

You may be fascinated by space travel, but have you ever thought about why the astronauts who take space walks wear meticulously engineered and designed spacesuits? It's not just because they need air to breathe. Once they venture beyond earth's atmosphere and magnetic field, a nuclear army is waiting to ambush them and destroy them in a second.

Two major enemies are in space: radioactive particles and waves that come from cosmic rays and solar radiation. Radioactive particles are generated by the explosions of supernovas and by giant stars that are composed of hydrogen, helium, and iron and release protons and alpha rays at nearly the speed of light. They could destroy the entire population of this earth in a microsecond.

We see the other source of deadly radiation every day—the sun. Sunshine is the result of an ongoing thermal-nuclear reaction that creates a solar flare that releases protons at ten billion times the rate of what is called a "solar wind." If one of those ever arrived on planet Earth, there would be no more planet Earth. But we've never been exposed to those although they happen all the time. Do you know why? Because of an invisible forcefield known as the planet's environmental shield. Earth is surrounded by a gas-filled atmosphere ringed by a two-part magnetic field called the "inner" and "outer" Van Allen belt, which basically forms an obstacle course that allows through only light and a few ultraviolet rays that give us our suntans.[3]

This is a God-created protective shield.

If God can protect our bodies from environmental dangers, don't you think he can and will protect our souls from eternal dangers? When you commit your soul and your eternal destiny to God, he's able to care for them. He's able to guard them. He's able to protect them today with the shield of resurrection power that's guarding your personal life.

And finally, there's a thrilling hope for our future.

## GOD GUIDES US TO ETERNAL LIFE

God takes care of our past by giving us spiritual life. God takes care of our present by guarding us in our personal life. And he takes care of our future because he's promised to guide us to eternal life.

As a believer, you've been born into God's family, God is your Father, and he has an inheritance for you. First Peter 1:4 says you will eventually enter "into an inheritance that can never perish, spoil or fade. This inheritance is kept in heaven for you." So this inheritance is not just heaven itself because it's *kept in* heaven. Do you know what your inheritance is? It's God himself.

Wait a minute, though. Heaven isn't for everybody.

The "you" in "this inheritance is kept in heaven for you" are those who have received spiritual life, who have been born again into God's family. To get into heaven we've got to have a reservation, and that reservation can be made only in the name of the risen Lord Jesus.

It amazes me how many people think they can do their own thing, live their own lives, go their own way, call their own shots, and then just show up at heaven's door and say, "Okay, God. I'm here. Open up." Let me say this as gently but as firmly as I can: If you think you can bypass Jesus, if you think you can live your life your way and still get into the presence of God, you're either incredibly arrogant or indisputably ignorant. Only God's children are allowed into God's house.

But once you've been given this spiritual life, once you become a child of God, you're guaranteed to get in. Why? Because God honors every reservation made in the name of his Son. That's a reservation that can never be canceled, and it's kept in God's safe-deposit box that no one can ever open but him.

I love what we're told about this inheritance, that it can never perish, spoil, or fade. Nothing can destroy it, nothing can defile it, nothing can displace it. It's ours forever. The Williams Group wealth consultancy conducted a study of wealthy families and found that "some 70 percent of well-to-do families lose their wealth by the second generation; by the third generation, 90 percent."[4] Well, not this inheritance. Once you have it, you can never lose it. It's yours forever.

———

We have this hope for our past, for our present, and for our future only because of a risen Lord. And only in two places in the universe is there no hope. One is hell, because if you go there, all hope is gone. The other is heaven, because in heaven there's no need for hope. But in the here and now, we need hope. It's beautiful to know that your tomorrow is taken care of, that you can handle the troubles of today and the heartaches of earth because you have a home in heaven.

The resurrection of Jesus is not a fairy tale; it's a fact that should control our feelings. If Jesus can answer the question of eternity, solve the problem of sin, and defeat the power of death, why should we ever let a subjective feeling overcome the objective truth that a risen Lord lives in us, fights for us, and one day will come for us?

I say it again: In these times we may feel helpless, but we are not hopeless! I declare to you that Jesus Christ is alive! Because of that, we have a living hope that's immune to every disease and impervious to every threat. It's a hope that never dies. And it's not just our best hope; it's our only hope.

Place your hope in the only One who makes hope a reality—the risen Savior. When you do, you'll experience the hope that, through him, you'll indeed deal with how you feel—and do it successfully!

# NOTES

## INTRODUCTION: EMOTION COMMOTION

1. "More Than 8 in 10 Americans (84%) Report Feeling Emotions Associated with Stress in the Last Two Weeks," *American Psychological Association*, January 2021, https://www.apa.org/images/sia-january-emotions-infographic_tcm7-283972.jpg.

2. "APA: U.S. Adults Report Highest Stress Level Since the Early Days of the COVID-19 Pandemic," *American Psychological Association*, February 2, 2021, https://www.apa.org/news/press/releases/2021/02/adults-stress-pandemic>.

3. Alasdair Groves, "Your Emotions Aren't the Most (or Least) Important Thing About You," *The Gospel Coalition*, May 6, 2019, https://www.thegospelcoalition.org/article/emotions-important/.

4. Groves, "Your Emotions Aren't the Most (or Least) Important Thing About You."

5. John Stott, *The Contemporary Christian* (Westmont, IL: IVP Press, 1992), 125.

6. Groves, "Your Emotions Aren't the Most (or Least) Important Thing About You."

7. "Social Media Fact Sheet," *Pew Research Center*, April 7, 2021, https://www.pewresearch.org/internet/fact-sheet/social-media/.

8. Don Colbert, M.D., *Deadly Emotions: Understand the Body-Mind-Spirit Connection That Can Heal or Destroy You* (Nashville, TN: Thomas Nelson, 2003), XI-XII.

## 1 | STRESS

1. "Shermanesque statement," *Political Dictionary*, https://politicaldictionary.com/words/shermanesque-statement/.

2. "The President's Many Roles," *Lumen*, https://courses.lumenlearning.com/boundless-political-science/chapter/the-presidents-many-roles/.

3. "Being president is bad for your health, study suggests," *BBC News*, December 15, 2015, https://www.BBC.com/news/health-35102077.

4. Eric Patterson, LPC, "Stress Facts and Statistics," *The Recovery Village*, updated August 5, 2021, https://www.therecoveryvillage.com/mental-health/stress/related/stress-statistics/.

5. Patterson, "Stress Facts and Statistics."

6. "Stress in America™ 2020," American Psychological Association, https://www.apa.org/news/press/releases/stress/2020/report.

7. "America's #1 Health Problem," The American Institute of Stress, https://www.stress.org/americas-1-health-problem.

8. Mary Elizabeth Dallas, "For Poorer Americans, Stress Brings Worse Health," *WebMD*, January 8, 2018, https://www.webmd.com/balance/stress-management/news/20180108/for-poorer-americans-stress-brings-worse-health.

9. "The Effects of Stress on Your Body," *WebMD*, December 14, 2019, https://www.webmd.com/balance/stress-management/effects-of-stress-on-your-body.

10. Don Colbert, M.D., *Deadly Emotions: Understand the Mind-Body-Spirit Connection That Can Heal or Destroy You* (Nashville, TN: Thomas Nelson, 2003), 25-27.

11. Os Guinness, *Impossible People* (Downers Grove, IL: IVP Books, 2016), 53.

12. Colbert, *Deadly Emotions*, 21.

13. Steve Farrar, *Tempered Steel* (Sisters, OR: Multnomah, 2012), 135.

14. Adapted from J.D. Greear, *Not God Enough* (Grand Rapids, MI.: Zondervan, 2018), 33.

15. Christian Standard Bible.

16. Chris Burke, "Positive and Negative Effects of Earthquakes," *Sciencing*, April 24, 2018, https://sciencing.com/facts-5497745-economic-impact-coastal-erosion.html.

17. E.J. Young, *The Book of Isaiah, Vol. III*, (Grand Rapids, MI.: Eerdmans, 1972), 68.

18. Ms. Jemi Sudhakar, "The Challenge of the Storm—The Eagle," August 22, 2017, https://www.linkedin.com/pulse/challenger-storm-eagle-ms-jemi-sudhakar-.

## 2 | WORRY

1. Ladan Nikravan Hayes, "The Fragile Emotional State of America," July 12, 2019, *Talkspace*, https://www.talkspace.com/blog/fragile-emotional-state-america/. Gallup's Annual Emotions Report surveyed more than 150,000 people in 140 countries to capture this data.

2. Kari Paul, "America's insomnia problem is even worse than before the great recession," MarketWatch, April 20, 2017, https://www.marketwatch.com/amp/stories/Americas-insomnia-problem-is-even-worse-than-before-the-Great-Recession-2017-04-20.

3. Zach Hrynowski, "66 Percent of Americans Remain Worried About Exposure to COVID-19," Gallup, June 17, 2020, https://www.news.gallup.com/polls/312680/Americans-remain-worried-exposure-Covid.asps.

4. This quote by Harold Stephens is cited by Zig Ziglar in his book *Life Lifters* (Nashville, TN: Broadman & Holman, 2003), 24.

5. Don Joseph Goewey, "85% of What We Worry About Never Happens," HuffPost, updated December 6, 2017, https://www.huffpost.com/entry/85-of-what-we-worry-about_b_8028368.

6. "New Study Doubles the Estimate of Bird Species in the World," American Museum of Natural History, December 2016, https://www.amnh.org/about/press-center/new-study-doubles-the-estimate-of-bird-species-in-the-world. "How Big Is the Bird Population?" American Museum of Natural History, https://www.amnh.org/explore/ology/earth/ask-a-scientist-about-our-environment/how-big-is-the-bird-population.

7. "Types of Lilies: A Visual Guide," FTD by Design, June 19, 2017, https://www.ftd.com/blog/share/types-of-lilies.

8. Shreya Dasgupta, "How many plant species are there in the world? Scientists now have an answer," *Mongabay*, May 12, 2016, https://ww.google.com/amps/s/news.mongabay.com/2016/05/mini-plants-world-scientists-may-now-answer/amp/.

9. Goewey, "85% of What We Worry About Never Happens."

10. https://www.vocabulary.com/dictionary/worry.

11. Quote Investigator, https://quoteinvestigator.com/2013/10/04/never-happened/.

12. Goewey, "85% of What We Worry About Never Happens."

13. Robert K. Storey, "Time to Let Go of Worry & Embrace the Peace of God," audio, FaithLife Sermons, https://sermons.faithlife.com/sermons/222471-time-to-let-go-of-worry-and-embrace-the-peace-of-god, first available February 10, 2010.

14. This is one version of a poem written by an unknown author.

## 3 | ANXIETY

1. National Institute of Mental Health, "Anxiety Disorders," https://www.nimh.nih.gov/health/topics/anxiety-disorders.

2. "Facts & Statistics," Anxiety & Depression Association of America, https://adaa.org/understanding-anxiety/facts-statistics.

3. Edmund J. Bourne, *The Anxiety & Phobia Workbook*, 6th ed. (Oakland, CA: New Harbinger, 2015), XI.

4. "Facts & Statistics," Anxiety & Depression Association of America, https://adaa.org/understanding-anxiety/facts-statistics/.

5. "New APA Poll Shows Surge in Anxiety Among Americans Top Causes Are Safety, COVID-19, Health, Gun Violence, and the Upcoming Election," American Psychiatric Association, October 21, 2020, https://www.psychiatry.org/newsroom/news-releases/anxiety-poll-2020.

6. Bourne, *The Anxiety & Phobia Workbook*, 1.

7. Xavia Malcolm, "Worry vs. Anxiety—What Is the Difference?" *Health Beat*, November 12, 2019, htpps://www.Jamaicahospital.org/newsletter/worry-vs-anxiety-what-is-the-difference/.

8. Henry Ford Health System Staff, "Worry and Anxiety: Do You Know the Difference?" *Henry Ford Livewell*, August 21, 2020, htpps://www.HenryFord.org/blog/2020/08/the-difference-between-worry-and-anxiety.

9. Earl Henslin, *This Is Your Brain on Joy* (Nashville, TN: Thomas Nelson Publishers, 2011). I accessed this information via https://www.iows.net/home.

10. https://www.studylight.org/language-studies/greek-thoughts.html?article=35.

11. Walter B. Knight, *Knight's Master Book of Illustrations* (Grand Rapids, MI: Eerdmans, 1956), 755.

12. Dr. Armand Nicholi Jr., *The Question of God: C.S. Lewis and Sigmund Freud Debate God, Love, Sex, and the Meaning of Life* (New York: Free Press, 2003), 105.

### 4 | DEPRESSION

1. David Shimer, "Yale's Most Popular Class Ever: Happiness," *The New York Times*, January 26, 2018, https://www.nytimes.com/2018/01/26/nyregion/at-yale-class-on-happiness-draws-huge-crowd-laurie-santos.html.

2. National Network of Depression Centers, https://nndc.org/facts "The Numbers Count: Mental Disorders in America," National Institute of Mental Health, https://www.nimh.nih.gov/health/publication/the-numbers-count-mental-orders-in-america/index.shtml; "CDC: Antidepressant Use Skyrockets 400% in Past Twenty Years," *USA Today*, October 10, 2011.

3. National Network of Depression Centers, https://nndc.org/facts/.

4. "Depression," Anxiety & Depression Association of America, https://adaa.org/understanding-anxiety/depression.

5. Bob Russell, *Jesus Lord of Your Personality* (West Monroe, LA: Howard Books, 2002), 103-104.

6. "Letter to John Stuart," The Railsplitter, https://housedivided.dickinson.edu/sites/lincoln/letter-to-john-stuart-january-23-1841/.

7. "Noise Sources and Their Effects," Purdue University, www.chem.purdue.edu/chemsafety/Training/PPETrain/dblevels.htm.

8. "Decibel Equivalent Tables: What Does Each Volume Sound Like?" housegrail.com/decibel-equivalent-table-whats-how-loud/.

9. "Noise Sources and Their Effects," Purdue University.

10. AZ Quotes, https://www.azquotes.com/author/9975-Karl_A_Menninger.

### 5 | FEAR

1. Argus Hamilton, "Clinton Proves George's Equal," *The Oklahoman*, September 30, 1998, https://www.oklahoman.com/article/2627922/clinton-proves-georges-equal.

2. John C. Maxwell, *Put Your Dream to the Test* (Nashville, TN: Thomas Nelson, 2011), 151.

3. "How Safe Are Elevators?" Elevator Injury Lawyer.com, https://www.elevatorinjurylawyer.com/common-accidents-and-injuries/how-safe-are-elevators/.

4. Brendan D'mello, "Why Are Elevator Safer Than You Thought?" December 2, 2019, https://www.scienceabc.com/innovation/how-safe-are-you-in-an-elevator.html.

5. Denis Waitley, *10 Seeds of Greatness* (Old Tappan, NJ: Fleming. H. Revell Co., 1983), 76.

6. Nelson L. Price, *Farewell to Fear* (Nashville, TN: Broadman Press, 1983), 53.

7. Tom Carter, compiler, *Spurgeon at His Best* (Grand Rapids, MI: Baker Books, 1988), 76.

### 6 | LONELINESS

1. Mark Jenkins, "America's most remote site—the undiscovered side of Yellowstone," August 25, 2016, https://www.theguardian.com/environment/2016/aug/25/yellowstone-national-park-wyoming-bears-wolves-remote.

2. Christine Peterson, "Battles with bears, nighttime rescues, most remote place in Lower 48 leaves its mark," updated October 29, 2015, *Casper Star Tribune*, https://trib.com/outdoors/battles-with-bears-nighttime-rescues-most-remote-place-in-lower-48-leaves-its-mark/article_13795327-939f-54f7-a733-648a031a4802.html.

3. "Cigna Takes Action to Combat the Rise of Loneliness and Improve Mental Wellness in America," January 23, 2020, https://newsroom.cigna.com/cigna-takes-action-to-combat-the-rise-of-loneliness-and-improve-mental-wellness-in-america.

4. "Dutch woman's dead body unnoticed in apartment for 10 years," UPI, November 24, 2013, https://www.upi.com/Top_News/World-News/2013/11/24/Dutch-womans-dead-body-unnoticed-in-apartment-for-10-years/12251385306410/; Grace Jauwena, "4 Ways to Tackle Loneliness," May 12, 2019, https://lifeandhealth.org/mindfulness/4-ways-to-tackle-loneliness/1515777.html.

5. Jauwena, "4 Ways to Tackle Loneliness."

6. "An epidemic of loneliness," *The Week*, January 6, 2019, https://theweek.com/articles/815518/epidemic-loneliness.

7. "The 'Loneliness Epidemic'," Health Resources & Services Administration, https://www.hrsa.gov/enews/past-issues/2019/january-17/loneliness-epidemic.

8. "An epidemic of loneliness," *The Week*, January 6, 2019, https://theweek.com/articles/815518/epidemic-loneliness.

9. Janelle Ringer, "Dealing with the mental health impact of social distancing," May 12, 2020, https://news.llu.edu/health-wellness/dealing-with-mental-health-impact-of-social-distancing.

10. "The 'Loneliness Epidemic,'" Health Resources & Services Administration, https://www.hrsa.gov/enews/past-issues/2019/january-17/loneliness-epidemic.

11. James Merritt, *52 Weeks Through the Psalms* (Eugene, OR: Harvest House, 2017), 192.

12. Adapted from https://www.pastorlife.com/members/sermon.asp?SERMON_ID=5317&USERID=&fm=whatnew.

13. R.C. Sproul, *Pleasing God* (Colorado Springs, CO: David C Cook, 2012), 148.

14. Tegan Cruyws and Genevieve Dingle, "Why lonely people visit the doctor more often," Psychlopaedia, November 15, 2018, https://psychlopaedia.org/health/why-lonely-people-visit-the-doctor-more-often/.

15. Kassandra I. Alcaraz, Katherine S. Eddens, Jennifer L. Blase, W. Ryan Diver, Alpa V. Patel, Lauren R. Teras, Victoria L. Stevens, Eric J. Jacobs, Susan M. Gapstur, "Social Isolation and Mortality in US Black and White Men and Women," *American Journal of Epidemiology*, Volume 188, Issue 1, January 2019, 102–109, academic.oup.com/aje/article/188/1/102/5133254.

16. *The Journals of Gerontology: Series B*, online 2018.

17. *Confident Living*, February 1990, 43.

18. Morris West, *The Devil's Advocate*, as quoted in J. Oswald Sanders, *Facing Loneliness* ebook (Grand Rapids, MI: Our Daily Bread Publishing, 2014).

## 7 | JEALOUSY

1. You can read the full story in *Mother Love, Deadly Love* by Anne McDonald Maier (New York, NY: St. Martin's Press, 1994).

2. Merriam-Webster, https://www.merriam-webster.com/dictionary/jealousy.

3. John Ortberg, *When the Game Is Over It All Goes Back in the Box* (Grand Rapids, MI: Zondervan, 2007), 38-39.

4. Charles R. Swindoll, *Living on the Ragged Edge* (Waco, TX: Word Books, 1985), 214.


## 8 | ANGER

1. Patricia Prijatel, "America the Angry," August 3, 2020, *Psychology Today*, https://www.psychology today.com/us/blog/all-is-well/202008/america-the-angry. Gallup's annual Global Emotions Report is from a survey of more than 150,000 people around the world.

2. Charles Duhigg, "The Real Roots of American Anger," *The Atlantic*, January/February Issue, https://www.theatlantic.com/magazine/archive/2019/01/charles-duhigg-american-anger/576424/.

3. Duhigg, "The Real Roots of American Anger."

4. Scott A. Bonn, PhD, "Fear-Based Anger Is the Primary Motive for Violence," *Psychology Today*, July 17, 2017, https://www.psychologytoday.com/us/blog/wicked-deeds/201707/fear-based-anger-is-the-primary-motive-violence.

5. Bonn, "Fear-Based Anger Is the Primary Motive for Violence."

6. https://science.howstuffworks.com/life/inside-the-mind/emotions/anger2.htm.

7. David DiSalvo, "Study: Anger and Heart Attacks Strongly Linked," June 9, 2013, https://www.forbes.com/search/?q=Anger%20and%20heart%20attacks&sh=6f8b056279f4.

8. Harry Mills, PhD, "Health Costs of Anger," *Gracepoint*, https://www.gracepointwellness.org/116-anger-management/article/5809-health-costs-of-anger.

9. Emma Young, "Do Get Mad: The Upside of Anger," *New Scientist*, February 6, 2013, https://www.newscientist.com/article/mg21729032-700-do-get-mad-the-upside-of-anger/.

10. Goodreads, https://www.goodreads.com/quotes/542189-we-praise-a-man-who-feels-angry-on-the-right.

11. Andrew Rotondi, "Billy Martin, Mickey Mantle, and the Cow Story," video, http://bronxpin stripes.com/yankees-history/billy-martin-mickey-mantle-and-the-cow-story/.

12. Quotefancy, https://quotefancy.com/quote/772881/Benjamin-Franklin-Take-it-from-Richard-poor-and-lame-What-s-begun-in-anger-ends-in-shame.

13. https://aleteia.org/2020/06/04/how-division-is-a-primary-tactic-of-the-devil/.

14. John 8:44: "He was a murderer from the beginning."

15. "Decapitated Snake Kills Chef," *The Atlanta-Journal Constitution*, August 26, 2014, https://www.ajc.com/news/decapitated-snake-kills-chef/Fty3VMukuHSHx2gMcxeiQN/.

16. (1999) Dead Snakes Can Still Bite, The Physician and Sportsmedicine, 27:8, 15, DOI: 10.3810/psm.1999.08.1657, https://www.tandfonline.com/doi/abs/10.3810/PSM.1999.08.1657.

## 9 | BITTERNESS

1. This story was told in an article by Timothy Roche, "A Cold Dose of Vengeance," *Time*, July 12, 1999, http://content.time.com/time/subscriber/article/0,33009,991455,00.html.

2. Don Colbert, MD, *Deadly Emotions* (Nashville, TN: Thomas Nelson, 2003), 135.

3. Kyle Idleman, *Grace Is Greater* (Grand Rapids, MI: Baker Books, 2017), 6.

4. Idleman, *Grace Is Greater*, 96.

5. "How to Beat Burnout," *Focus on the Family*, CS315/1090/1999.

6. Anson R. Nash Jr., *He Who Laughs Last, Lasts* (Maitland, FL: Xulon Press, 2004), 113.9, citing *Holy Humor*, Cal and Rose Samra, *Guideposts*, 1995, 120.

7. Clip from *The Andy Griffith Show*, YouTube, https://www.youtube.com/watch?v=gU5iLiEySyk.

8. Dave Stone, "Ten Years Later: Love Prevails," sermon, Southeast Christian Church, Louisville, Kentucky, September 11, 2011, www.southeastchristian.org/default.aspx.

9. Harold W. Hoener, *Ephesians An Exegetical Commentary* (Grand Rapids, MI: Baker, 2002), 636.

10. Laura Hillebrand, *Unbroken* (New York, NY: Random House, 2010), 396-397.

## 10 | GUILT

1. Lauran Neergaard and Yu Bing, "Doctors remove knife from man's head after four years," CBS8, February 18, 2011, https://www.cbs8.com/article/news/doctors-remove-knife-from-mans-head-after-4-years/509-ea86eb60-25c8-4078-bb0e-ddf0be4be822.

2. James Montgomery Boice, *Psalms (An Expositional Commentary)* (Grand Rapids, MI: Baker Books, 1996),426.

3. http://helpmewithbiblestudy.org/8Sin/NatureIniquity.aspx.

4. https://www.patheos.com/blogs/e2medianetwork/2016/11/wwutt-sin-means-to-miss-the-mark/.

5. Tony Reinke, "Lecrae Confesses Abortion, Invites Others into the Light," *DesiringGod*, January 17, 2015, https://www.desiringgod.org/articles/lecrae-confesses-abortion-invites-others-into-the-light.

6. Max Lucado, *A Gentle Thunder: Hearing God Through the Storm* (Nashville, TN: Thomas Nelson, 1995, reprint edition 2012), 173.

7. I got this thought from Max Lucado, *No Wonder They Call Him the Savior* (Portland, OR: Multnomah, 1986), 139-140.

8. https://www.bibleref.com/Psalms/51/Psalm-51-7.html. Which is exactly the way the *ESV* translates it.

9. The same word *bara'* is used in both places.

## 11 | FAITH

1. Philip Edgecumbe Hughes, *A Commentary on the Epistle to the Hebrews* (Grand Rapids, MI: Eerdmans, 1977), 439; See also Paul Ellington, *NIGNT Commentary on Hebrews* (Grand Rapids, MI: Eerdmans, 1993), 564.

2. Steven Pinker, "Less Faith, More Reason," *The Harvard Crimson,* October 27, 2006, https://www.thecrimson.com/article/2006/10/27/less-faith-more-reason-there-is/.

3. Ellington, *NIGHT Commentary on Hebrews,* 565.

4. Greg Stielstra, *PyroMarketing: The Four-Step Strategy to Ignite Customer Evangelism and Keep Them for Life* (New York, NY: Harper Business, 2005), 92.

## 12 | JOY

1. Walt Disney World Statistics, https://magicguides.com/disney-world-statistics/, accessed August 30, 2021.

2. "List of Countries by GDP," Wikipedia, https://en.wikipedia.org/wiki/List_of_countries_by_GDP_(nominal). See also https://magicguides.com/disney-world-statistics/.

3. Jeremy Brown, "At the Happiest Place on Earth, even the little things bring big smiles," *Fatherly,* July 20, 2018, https://ww.google.com/amp/s/www.fatherly.com/play/100moments-at-walt-disney-world-that-inspire-pure-joy/amp/. Emphasis added.

4. Craig Brian Larson and Phyllis Ten Elshof, *1001 Illustrations That Connect* (Grand Rapids, MI: Zondervan 2008), 74; Joni Eareckson Tada, "Joy Hard Won," *Decision,* March 2000.

5. Dave Caswell, "Our Father, Who does art in heaven, Harold is His name," Waterhouse Ridge Memory Care Blog, July 26, 2016, https://www.waterhouseridge.com/senior-living/or/beaverton/blog/cazzy-s-corner-our-father-who-does-art-in-heaven-harold-is-his-name.

6. Randy Harvey, "He Was a '10' at the Movies as Well as on the Field," *Los Angeles Times,* July 28, 1997, https://www.latimes.com/archives/la-xpm-1997-jul-28-sp-17106-story.html.

7. BrainyQuotes, https://www.brainyquote.com/quotes/zig_ziglar_381984.

8. John C. Maxwell, *Thinking for a Change* (New York, NY: Warner Books, 2003).

## 13 | GRATITUDE

1. Mike Durbin, "A 100-dollar Word," *Baptist Beacon,* November 4, 2020, https://www.baptistbeacon.net/post/a-100-dollar-word.

2. Heather Creekmore, "Man Sues His Parents for Creating Him," *CareNet,* February 21, 2019, https://www.care-net.org/abundant-life-blog/man-sues-his-parents-for-creating-him.

3. Geeta Pandey, "Indian man to sue parents for giving birth to him," February 7, 2019, *BBC News, Delhi,* https://www.bbc.com/news/world-asia-india-47154287.

4. Literally *En Panti* F.F. Bruce, *1 & 2 Thessalonians Word Biblical Commentary* (Waco, TX: Word Books, 1982), 124.

5. Randy Alcorn, *Money, Possessions and Eternity* (Wheaton, IL: Tyndale, 1989), 19-120.

6. Jamie Ducharme, "7 Surprising Health Benefits of Gratitude," *Time,* November 20, 2017, https://time.com/5026174/health-benefits-of-gratitude.

7. Robert Emmons, "Why Gratitude Is Good," *Greater Good Magazine,* November 16, 2010, https://greatergood.berkeley.edu/article/item/why gratitude_is_good.

8. Mark Batterson, *Double Blessing: How to Get It and How to Give It* (Colorado Springs, CO: Multnomah, 2019), 94.

9. "Blessed," www.sermonillustrator.org/illustrator/sermon2/blessed.htm.

10. Fran Tarkenton, *What Losing Taught Me About Winning* (New York, NY: Simon & Shuster, 1997), 165-166.

11. Jacqueline Howard, "The bizarre psychology of the bronze medal win," *CNN*, August 18, 2016, https://www.cnn.com/2016/08/18/health/bronze-medal-psychology-olympics/index.html.

12. Leah Hall, "58 Gratitude Quotes to Bring Joy to Every Day," *Country Living*, August 23, 2021, https://www.countryliving.com/life/g28564406/gratitude-quotes/.

## 14 | CONTENTMENT

1. Patrick McGinnis, "How FOMO Was Created," *Harvard Business Review*, December 19, 2019, https://hbr.org/podcast/2019/12/season-3-finale-how-fomo-was-created.

2. Margaret Rhodes, "Yes, FOMO Is Now a Word in the Dictionary," *Fast Company*, August 30, 2013, https://www.fastcompany.com/3016488/yes-fomo-is-now-a-word-in-the-dictionary.

3. Kent Carlson and Mike Lueken, *Renovation of the Church* (Hillgrove, IL: IVP Books, 2011), 116.

4. "500 Greatest Songs of All Time," *Rolling Stone*, December 11, 2003, https://www.rollingstone.com/music/music-lists/500-greatest-songs-of-all-time-151127/smokey-robinson-and-the-miracles-shop-around-71184/.

5. Dave Tompkins, Music Database, "VH1—100 Greatest Rock Songs," https://www.cs.ubc.ca/~davet/music/list/Best15.html.

6. "Why 85% of people hate their jobs," *Staff Squared HR*, December 3, 2019, https://www.staffsquared.com/blog/why-85-of-people-hate-their-jobs/.

7. Dietrich Muller, "maqhths," *The New International Dictionary of New Testament Theology* 1:483.

8. "Turkey," *American Culture*, https://amcultclass.weebly.com/turkey.html.

9. Dan Miller, "The Unhappy Farmer—A Story About Contentment," as told on Better Life Coaching Blog, October 24, 2014, https://betterlifecoaching.wordpress.com/2014/10/24/the-unhappy-farmer-a-story-about-contentment/.

## 15 | HOPE

1. John C. Maxwell, *Developing the Leaders Around You* (Nashville, TN: Nelson Business, 2005), 72.

2. Chet Scott, "Air Force Three," *Heartbeat International*, https://www.heartbeatservices.org/air-force-three.

3. Kenneth Kamler, *Surviving the Extremes* (New York, NY: St. Martin's Press, 2004), 260-261.

4. Jeff Wuorio, "How to avoid being the 70 percent who squander their inheritance," *Deseret News*, September 4, 2016, https://www.deseret.com/2016/9/4/20595426/how-to-avoid-being-the-70-percent-who-squander-their-inheritance#it-may-be-surprising-but-even-substantial-inheritances-can-be-lost-through-mistakes-and-oversights-if-you-come-into-money-here-are-some-strategies-to-handle-it-intelligently.

# ACKNOWLEDGMENTS

A book may have one author, but invariably it's the result of a behind-the-scenes team. My team is first class.

It begins and ends with the love of my life, Teresa, who has been by my side for four and a half decades and counting. She's still the one, and she always will be.

Jonathan is my agent, my editor, my proofreader, and a beloved son. I can only wish I were a fraction of the writer and wordsmith he is, but you can't have or be everything. Thanks, son, for loving me enough to work with me and walk with me in the publishing world.

My team at Harvest House is a joy to work with, and Bob Hawkins is a five-star friend and partner. I'm so thankful they think me worthy to put their brand on my book.

Thanks to my church, Cross Pointe, for your love for me and for God's Word. You make pastoring and preaching such a joy!

Then thanks to my faithful assistant, Kalli, whose suggestions, corrections, and ultimately production made this book not only possible but a whole lot better after her sharp eye and deft hand polished it all up! You are the best.

Finally, I'm so grateful to the God who gave his truth in the book that gives us the one and only repository of divine advice on how to deal with how we feel. Without his book, you wouldn't be reading this one!

# OTHER HARVEST HOUSE BOOKS BY JAMES MERRITT

9 Ways to Hold On When You Want to Give Up

52 Weeks with Jesus

52 Weeks with Jesus Devotional

52 Weeks Through the Bible

52 Weeks Through the Bible Devotional

52 Weeks Through the Psalms

52 Weeks Through the Psalms Devotional

Character Still Counts

God, I've Got a Question

The 25 Days of Christmas

To learn more about Harvest House books and
to read sample chapters, visit our website:

**www.HarvestHousePublishers.com**

**HARVEST HOUSE PUBLISHERS**
EUGENE, OREGON